SOURCE TO SEA

A 2,000-MILE CANOE JOURNEY DOWN THE MISSISSIPPI RIVER

JOHN PUGH

PHOTOGRAPHY BY
JESSICA ROBINSON

FREE BONUS E-BOOK!

READ THIS FIRST

As a token of appreciation for reading my book, I would like to offer you a 100% free bonus e-book.

It's filled with exclusive content, journals, and photos.

DOWNLOAD YOUR FREE BONUS E-BOOK at

https://BookHip.com/QHZBXKW

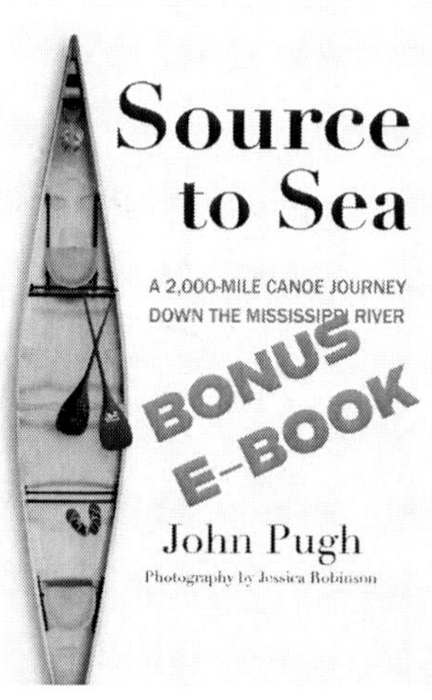

Visit **www.SourcetoSea.net** for more information on our Mississippi River adventure, Appalachian Trail thru-hike, and additional bonus material.

PRAISE FOR SOURCE TO SEA

"John tells a story of our great river through a lens that we can all relate to - the adventure of paddling 2,000 miles coupled with the adventure of our partner, and we can see how they both change us forever, for the better."

Andrew Downs, Executive Director, New River Conservancy

"Follow along as John and Jessica take you on an incredible source to sea journey down the Mississippi River. Their tale is a comprehensive and detailed look at what it is to paddle the Mississippi River and take on the adventure of a lifetime. Part guidebook, part diary, part history tome, and part DIY how-to/what-not-to-do story. There's drama, there's comedy, there's laughter and tears, there are many surprises, and it's always interesting. This book has a little bit of everything and all the right stuff. I didn't want to put it down, and I don't think you will either."

Dan Faust, 2-time Mississippi River S2S paddler, Missouri River S2S, and crew for World Record holder Dale "Grey Beard" Sanders.

"As a fellow paddler of one of America's greatest rivers, I have to say that reading this book brought back a flood of memories. Stories of those first anxious days on the river, storms, battling the winds, alligators on the Atchafalaya, all this took me back to the river. Many thanks to John and Jess for sharing their journey with us."

Andy Bugh, Mississippi River S2S paddler

"A page turner from the very beginning. I felt like I was in the canoe with them. I got to experience all the adventure with none of the mosquitoes!"

C. Newton, Independent Review

ISBN 978061526733-3 (paperback)

ISBN 9798269062907 (hardcover)

For an extended gear list, journals, and additional bonus material, visit
www.SourcetoSea.net

"Travel is fatal to prejudice, bigotry, and narrow-mindedness, and many of our people need it sorely on these accounts. Broad, wholesome, charitable views of men and things cannot be acquired by vegetating in one little corner of the earth all one's lifetime."
    -Mark Twain

FOREWORD

The Mississippi River. "Big Muddy, Mighty Mississippi, Father of Waters, Mark Twain" and all that stuff. That big blue line right in the middle of the United States map. Can't miss it.

Before we started, the Mississippi was more concept than reality for me. I'd only seen it once before. When I was about eleven, we drove out to visit one of my stepdad's old army buddies in Missouri. They had a farm next to the river. Thousands of acres, big tractors, and all that stuff. We rode around and looked at the river, but it didn't hit home for me. I guess I was way more into my comics and crosswords.

The river is a lot of things. It's a means of conveyance and commerce, a way to move goods and people for hundreds of miles. It was a route for slaves to escape the South, and a highway for the convergence of ideas, food, music, and cultures.

It's been both a connector and a divider for millennia: trading posts, forts, boundaries. There's a reason phrases like "Highest Point East of the Mississippi" or "Biggest Hairball West of the Mississippi" exist.

It's an enormous resource, taking in the waters of 31 states and two Canadian provinces. That's about 41% of the continental United States, covering around 1.5 million square miles. If you look at a watershed map, you realize just how massive this watershed really is.

According to our friends at the Audubon Society and the USGS, the Mississippi is home to at least 260 fish species. That's 25% of all fish species in North America, if you're into the math stuff. Sixty percent (326 species) of North American migratory birds use it as a flyway. The river also hosts more than 50 mammal species, including more than 70 million people living in its watershed. That's a lot of mammals.

If you combine the lengths of the Missouri and Mississippi rivers, they're the fourth-longest river system in the world, behind the Nile, Amazon, and Yangtze.

But it's not all smooth sailing. The Mississippi has been dealing with issues such as Asian carp, eutrophication in the Dead Zone, and agricultural and industrial pollution for decades.

I'd be remiss if I didn't mention the Atchafalaya River.

It flows from the Red River, winding into the Gulf of Mexico. It's small, swampy, wild, and remote, and insanely beautiful. We loved it. It was the perfect route for us to finish the trip.

For us, the Mississippi went from concept to reality over about 2,150 miles. We still often talk about this trip, and it influences many of the things we do today. We collected a small jar of water on the last day on the river and keep it in a kitchen cabinet. I'll give it a shake every now and then, and it always brings a smile.

So here's our story of 73 days paddling down the river. Mostly good, some bad, a little ugly—but all of it real.

-John Pugh
September 20, 2025

CONTENTS

PART ONE
HEADWATERS TO MINNEAPOLIS

IT'S TIME
BEMIDJI, MINNESOTA - MILE 0

"YOU ARE LISTENING TO NATIONAL WEATHER SERVICE RADIO STATION WXM 99.... HERE'S THE WEATHER SUMMARY. COLD CONDITIONS WILL CONTINUE WITH SNOW SHOWERS AND LIGHT RAIN. LOWS 30-35, HIGHS IN THE MID-40S, WINDS 15 TO 20 MILES PER HOUR."

The crackling, digital voice from the weather radio brought little good news, but after a year of planning and stress, it's time to go. Rain, sleet, snow, or gloom of night be damned.

The sun's coming up, and we've been up most of the night, repacking gear one last time. We're both running on nerves and adrenaline. More than anything, I just want to get on the river. I don't care if we only paddle two miles. At least the trip will finally be underway.

Yesterday, every car and truck we saw was towing a boat. Old boats. New boats. Everything-In-Between-Boats. It's officially Walleye Season in Minnesota.

Fishing is more of a religion than recreation up here. We were in the lobby when a few guys straggled back in the middle of the night. It was freezing cold and raining, and these dudes were chasing walleye. There's always a flotilla of boats ready to drop lines the second the clock hits midnight. Like I said, it's a religion here, and these folks take it seriously.

All the planning, organizing, and chasing sponsorships. Packing, repacking, and re-repacking. Then, finally, we schlepped our canoe and gear halfway across the country.

Now we're here.

The river is small and shallow for the first sixty miles, and there are going to be plenty of downed trees left over from the winter. It actually flows north for a while before turning south again, like a big question mark. Seems appropriate. Hardly anyone's paddled this stretch this year. Hell, there was ice on the water a few weeks ago.

Sign at the Mississippi River Source

We're packing as little as possible to make it through. If the river's low, you stand a good chance of doing more hiking than paddling. I love to hike, but not while dragging a canoe full of gear behind me. We're hoping the rain will raise the river level and make things more manageable. Whatever.

This isn't a sprint.
It's a marathon.
One stroke at a time.
It's time.

WANAGAN LANDING, MINNESOTA, MILE 5

Today. Was. Amazing.

The months of planning and dreaming are finally behind us. Now we can just concentrate on doing the thing. I feel like a huge weight's off my shoulders, maybe replaced with another. I'm sure our lovely and ever-so-benevolent drivers, Candace (Jess's mom) and our long-time buddy Donald, were ready to abandon us, too. It's been a long few days.

Itasca State Park was created in 1891 to protect the surrounding pine forests from logging. The Civilian Conservation Corps built many of the current facilities in the 1930s, including the small rock dam where the river begins its journey to the Gulf.

At the start, the Mississippi is about fifteen feet wide and barely a foot deep—you could jump across it if you wanted to. Several kids ran back and forth across a log bridge while we were loading the canoe. I wonder if they knew how big this little creek gets or where it ends up?

I can't get my head around it going two-thousand-something miles, but I'm sure these kids weren't too worried about it.

Kids crossing the Mississippi

Getting on the water today puts us ahead of schedule. I say "schedule" loosely because there's no way to know where we'll be on any given date. There are too many things to consider, and trying to stick too tightly to a schedule is madness. That said, we've got a deadline. We've got to be back by the time classes resume in mid-August. That gives us about 90 days at the most to do the trip, pack up, travel back to North Carolina, unpack, and prep for reentry back into the real world. It is what it is.

No matter what happens, I'm happy we made a go of it. Sharing your dreams with the world is terrifying, but worth it. The first step is always the hardest. Everything else is gravy now.

I walked over to the lake to gather my thoughts and took a good luck drink. The water was so cold it made my teeth hurt. Candace gave us a monster bag of Twizzlers, and man, those things are delicious.

Canoe just before putting in at Lake Itasca Headwaters

I thought of something right after we pushed off. Even though Jess and I have paddled a bunch of whitewater and taught kayak and canoe classes, we've never been in a canoe *together*. We've always been in separate boats with other people or paddled solo.

I believe they call that *a tactical error*.

A quarter mile downstream, the river flows through a five-foot-wide culvert. Jess pushed the canoe in, while Donald and I caught it at the other end. One of his shoes got soaked in the effort. I owe him for that, among several hundred other things he's done over the years. He and his wife, Britt, are some of my closest friends. They've seen me at my best and worst—and still put up with me. Love them to death.

Most of our gear is squeaky clean right now. The canoe has never touched water, except for being rained on during the drive up. I ran my hand over it just before we took it off the car rack. So smooth. I almost felt guilty about the scratches it's going to have soon. The dry bags still have that new car smell. Yeah, that's not going to last long.

We'll use our cheap, heavy, indestructible backup paddles for this first stretch. More like battle axes than surgical tools, but we don't want to tear up the nice paddles with all the shallow water and rocks. We'll pick up the bent shaft paddles and extra gear when we get to Bemidji.

We had heavy winds, rain, and sleet for the first few miles. The sleet would bounce off the aluminum paddle shafts, making this weird little 'ting' sound. It's cute until an ice pellet smacks you in the face.

Ting!

Giggle

Ouch!

After a few hours of steady rain, we were ready to pull over for the night. The Minnesota Department of Natural Resources has designated the Mississippi River as a paddle trail and has marked campsites from here to Minneapolis. Although it's only five miles from where we started, we looked around every bend in the river until we arrived at Wanagan Landing.

We were wet and freezing and needed to dry off and eat before we turned into ice cubes. Jess made hot chocolate and pasta while I shuttled gear and set up the tent. We dove in and took a nap while the wind died down.

The air up here is crisp, cold, and smells like spruce pine. It reminds me of backpacking in the Great Smoky Mountains and the highlands in the Mount Rogers National Recreation Area. God, I love that scent. Brings back a lot of memories of waking up to damp fog and frosty mornings.

Frosty Canoe

We've seen a ton of wildlife up here. Bald eagles, mink, otters, ducks, swans, great blue herons, pipers, red-winged blackbirds, turtles, hawks, and several other critters I didn't get a good look at. Sometimes we'd round a bend and see swans with their babies (cygnets) swimming just in front of the canoe, peep-peep-peeping along.

Jess and I have spent dozens of nights in the woods together, but never on a trip this long.

This afternoon, it finally hit me.

We're in Minnesota.

We've got a long way to go.

We feel like the luckiest kids in the world out here.

May 15, 2005

LETTING GO

The river splits into countless branches as it flows through the wetlands. Some peter out into nothing, while others slip under floating bogs of cattails and rushes. As the river level changes, the bogs break and form new routes. For the most part, you pick your way through as best you can. The only clue to follow is the rivergrass growing at the bottom of the stream bed. The grasses bend with the current and point the way downstream.

At one point, we followed a dead-end channel and had to work our way over to where we thought the river *might* be. We pushed, shoved, and dragged the canoe through the marsh until we finally found the channel again. Trudging through the cold mud made me thankful for the dry socks waiting for me when we reached camp.

We have a map, compass, and GPS, but these are useless when the river changes so dynamically. Sometimes, you need to let go of being in control and *just follow the rivergrass.*

It's that damn simple, and I need to remember that.

Just follow the rivergrass

BEAR DEN LANDING CAMPSITE, MINNESOTA, MILE 30

It's 11 a.m., and we've covered about eight miles. Chilly morning. Woke up to frost and frozen fingers. We didn't bring enough cold-weather paddling gear with us, and it's biting us in our frozen butts. Yeah, I'm a wuss. I can't wait for it to warm up.

Man, this campsite is trashed. Hacked-off deer hooves still frozen from winter deer hunting season, broken beer bottles, toilet paper, and crap behind every tree, etc. We've been here 20 minutes, and it's weird. Creepy. Time to get out. I hate to poop and run, but...

We've seen maybe six people in the last three days. One guy was fishing off a bridge. Bold and cold. Fish on, dude. Save some for the rest of us.

There are critters everywhere—lots of birds: pipers, red-winged blackbirds, eagles, and our friends, the Canada geese. Canada geese are the drama queens of the river. Most birds fly off and mind their business when they see us. Not Canada geese. No, these things raise a colossal racket when they take off—honk, honk, honking, forever honking. They're honking a half mile away. Then, honking some more. Canada geese are obnoxious, but also kind of amazing.

My left shoulder feels like somebody is shoving an icepick through it, and I'm popping ibuprofen like candy. I'm sure that's doing wonders for my kidneys. Hope that goes away soon.

How Did We End Up on the Mississippi River?

I've always loved talking to folks about the long chain of events that led them to a particular place or moment. Changing just one or two things can lead a person down a wildly different path. My story starts with two ponds back in Climax, North Carolina.

The first pond was at Albert Fields' place, across the dirt road from where I grew up. We had a little creek running through our land for the cows, but Mr. Fields had a good-sized pond. Playing in the creek was fun, but it's tough to backstroke in three inches of water.

I used to go down there to fish for catfish with this god-awful smelling concoction I made out of liver, parmesan cheese, and whatever spices I could sneak from Mom's kitchen. I'd mix it up and let it sit in the sun for a few days. That bait was murder on catfish, if it didn't kill you first. The first whiff when you opened the Cool Whip container could burn the hair right out of your nose.

A bunch of kids from around here would go swimming there too. In the dog days of summer, you had to shoo cows out of the way and slog through mud and cow pies to get to the water. Eventually, they'd wander off to the other side of the pond and ignore the racket.

The second pond was at Quaker Lake Camp, just four miles down the road, though it felt a world away. That's where I learned to swim and paddle a canoe for the first time. Got my first kiss from a young lady named Betty there, behind the Arts & Crafts hut after the Friday night campfire. I'm pretty sure it wasn't *her* first kiss, though.

During canoeing class, we'd drag big aluminum canoes off the rack and into the lake. We spent hours paddling in circles, running into shore, and swamping boats for fun. Our hippie counselors from Guilford College were saints to deal with the chaos. At the end of each week, we'd practice canoe rescues. The lake wasn't that deep, and I can still feel the goo on the bottom oozing between my toes.

Those camp experiences led to earning my canoeing merit badge at Boy Scout camp. From there, I started paddling more during weekend trips and eventually became a High Adventure Director at another Scout camp.

Some of Jess's first water memories were alongside Little Beaver Creek in northeastern Ohio. The creek park had a swinging bridge, plenty of rocks to skip, and an ancient water pump. Grumman aluminum canoes are also employed for memories of first paddling and camping with family. Jess was always amazed by the big storms that would flood the streets of Lisbon, watching people wade and swim in the floodwaters.

After moving outside urban Columbus, Jess still found ways to be near water. A drainage ditch that fed into an industrial retention pond became the site of daily jumping contests between her and her brother, Rich. They spent hours wading in Alum Creek and floating downstream after heavy rains, bumping over downed trees and fighting the current. Probably not the safest pastime, but feeling the pull of moving water awakens something in a lot of us, doesn't it?

Later, she spent summers at Camp Oty'okwa, a Big Brothers Big Sisters camp in Hocking Hills. She went for at least two weeks every summer for ten years—first as a camper, then a counselor-in-training, junior staff, and finally as a counselor. Surrounded by creeks and streams, the camp hiked out to surrounding state parks and followed drainages that weave through the hills, passing many sandstone and limestone formations, providing opportunities for a splash and swim. The camp ran canoe trips on the Hocking River, and she progressed from paddling to leading trips. One summer, when her canoe instructor was laid up with a herniated disc, she ran the same few-mile stretch outside of Logan, Ohio, up to five days a week as the Adventure Program Coordinator for teens.

She was encouraged to study Adventure Recreation at Ohio University in Athens, about 40 miles downstream from camp. At first, her paddling skills didn't stand out among the more seasoned members of OU's whitewater program. She spent more time swimming than she planned to, but those early dunks helped her build the skills and judgment that would last a lifetime.

After undergrad, she joined AmeriCorps NCCC, where she promised herself to do more real paddling. She was enticed to come back as a Master's Teaching Assistant by my friend Matt Zuefle, where she met me, and everything went downstream - so to speak.

One of my old professors from UNC Greensboro, Matt Zuefle, had taken a job at Ohio University. When I finished my thru-hike, Matt asked about my plans. I told him, "Man, I just walked 2,100 miles and have twenty bucks to my name. My calendar's pretty wide open." "Dude! Come up to Ohio for grad school. We'll drink beers. You might learn something," he replied. So I did, and that's where Jess and I first met.

We helped lead a week-long adventure trip to the Okefenokee Swamp and Cumberland Island National Seashore. Driving back after a few days in the swamp, we decided to do a really long paddle trip together sometime. We weren't even dating yet. We looked at a map, saw this thin blue line meandering from Minnesota to the Gulf of Mexico, and that was that.

Iron Bridge Campsite, Minnesota

MILE 41

I'm sitting on a bluff overlooking the river, taking in a panoramic view of the valley we just paddled through. It's a long valley ringed by spruce, pine, and birch trees, with the river winding through it. When I'm backpacking, I like to look back and see the mountains I've hiked over all day. Seeing the ridges with a tiny footpath meandering through always blows me away. I tend to lose sight of the forest for the trees. Today, I'm glad for the view.

These last few days have been incredible. Quiet. Wild. Cold. We've paddled forty miles and have about fifteen more to reach Bemidji. I still can't believe we're finally doing this. We've talked about this for three years, and here we are. It's crazy.

While eating dinner, I thought about all the food preparation we've done. I wish I had weighed all the pasta, jerky, fruit bars, peanut butter, and other stuff piled in our living room before we mailed our resupply packages. We easily had 200 pounds of food, and we'll eat every crumb, and then some.

Iron Bridge Campsite, MN

Jess and I will each burn around 5,000 calories a day while we're out here. To balance that out, we'll be eating constantly—shoveling in food at every opportunity. The canoe lets us carry a variety of foods—fresh, canned, dried, and, most importantly, a lot of it.

We usually only cook one late-afternoon meal, though Jess may need a coffee in the morning to get moving. I've got a brutal soda addiction and dread the caffeine withdrawal, but I plan to suffer through it and just drink water. That pledge will last until we reach Bemidji, where I shall drink straight from the first soda fountain. We all have our demons.

The sun is setting and reflecting on the river in front of me. I'd take a picture, but it's pointless. There's no way I can capture the red, yellow, purple, orange, and blue sky with a camera.

Some pictures are better left in the mind.

May 16, 2005

~

TWENTY YEARS LATER - WHAT WAS I REALLY FEELING?

Exhaustion. *Total, pure exhaustion.*

We'd spent a year wrapping up a million details—juggling classes, writing sponsors, gathering gear, and subletting our apartment, on top of everything else. By the time we hit the water, I was a piping hot mess.

Nervous? Hell yeah, I was nervous. We'd never done anything this big, and I was overthinking everything possible as usual.

Oh yeah—I was also writing a series of newspaper articles to help pay for the trip and had a decent-sized email list following along, so if we screwed up, a whole bunch of people would know about it in real time.

I put on my smiling face and bullshitted outward confidence, but man, I was a train wreck. Jess is a saint to put up with me on a good day. This was a regular day times 1,000. I'm sure that was fun for her to deal with. Sorry, babe.

BEMIDJI, MINNESOTA
MILE 55

We made it through the first stretch and haven't killed each other—I'll take that as a good sign. Jess and I have gotten along great, and we're really starting to gel. Some people call canoes "Divorce Machines." I mean, I can see where they're coming from, but so far, so good.

The river stays in one channel now instead of branching off like in the wetlands. It's about thirty feet across, flows well, and is easy to follow. Earlier, we had to dodge, duck under, or drag the canoe over several trees in the river. Just straightforward grunt work. Builds character, so they say.

Coming from the backpacking world, I've heard plenty of complaints about the lack of maintenance in the backcountry. I don't think folks realize how stretched agencies already are, especially with budget shortfalls and personnel shortages. Volunteers do much of the maintenance in many areas, so I'm grateful for whatever they can manage. It's the outdoors, not a freeway, right?

Birds at Sunset

A dog wandered out of the woods and hung out with us this morning. For the next hour, he ran alongside us and swam back and forth across the river at least a dozen times. He was wearing dog tags and wasn't worried about getting lost. I bet he knows these woods like the back of his paw.

The wind picked up as we approached Lake Irving just outside of town. I talked Jess into going straight across the lake to the bridge that connects to Lake Bemidji instead of skirting the shore. My bright idea was to save time so we could get to town and celebrate.

Ok, I have a lot of stupid ideas.

We switched things up and put me in the bow to provide more power up front while Jess steered from the stern. Three hundred yards from shore, the whole thing fell apart. I'm sure Jess figured this out well before I did. The weight balance was way out of whack, and she's a much better bow paddler than I am anyway.

The wind whipped up waves, so we had to paddle directly into them to avoid capsizing. That was fine, except the wind blew us away from that opening in the dam separating the two lakes. We ended up about a mile from where we wanted to be when we finally got across. We had to follow the shore, duck under the bridge, and work our way around to the dock by the visitor center.

Nice shortcut, dude.

The lake was a mess as we worked back towards the bridge. It was cold, and we were in no mood to capsize so close to the end. We paddled broadside to the waves and shoreline, then finally reached the edge of the dock and turned towards shore.

The waves lapped at the gunnels, but we kept most of the water out. We hit the beach, stashed the gear under a tree, and came back for the canoe. It was like wrestling with an eighteen-foot kite, but we finally managed to turn it over and tied to some trees. Done! It was time to relax and eat everything in sight.

A twenty-foot statue of Paul Bunyan and Babe the Blue Ox greeted us as we walked into Bemidji.

Paul Bunyon and Babe the Blue Ox, Bemidji, MN

After a couple of burgers at The Keg and Cork, we started to feel human again. We've been on the river for less than a week, and I already feel like I could eat the south end of a northbound horse.

We'll be seeing a bunch of lakes over the next few weeks. We can go straight across in calm conditions or paddle the long way around by the shore if the wind whips up. Dawn is usually the best time to cross, so we'll need to be ready to move early. We'll have to plan a few days ahead to juggle the lakes, weather, and available campsites.

We're finally on the river, heading to the Gulf of Mexico some 2,300 miles away. I still can't wrap my head around it. All we can do is take every day as it comes. We're feeling good and ready to see what's next.

May 18, 2005

THE NEXT DAY...

We're sitting in a coffee shop watching the world go by. I just had a spinach burrito for breakfast, and I'm already eyeing the lunch menu. Today's going to be a good day.

Earlier, a group of moms had six kids in tow. They were oblivious to their children bouncing off the walls, so I grabbed a guitar from the corner in a doomed attempt to calm the savage beasts. I can't say it did much, but it felt good to noodle around a bit. I thought about buying a small travel guitar before the trip but decided it would just be one more thing to keep dry. Probably scare the critters off anyway.

There's still tons of wind, making Lake Bemidji a frothy soup of white-capped waves. We have to pick up groceries and supplies anyway, so we have a good excuse to take the day off. Worst-case scenario, we'll skirt the shore tomorrow instead of crossing the lake. We'll just have to wait and see what the weather brings.

Bemidji State University's Outdoor Pursuits Program put us up for the night. Showers and a dry floor to sleep on—can't ask for more than that. We stored some extra gear at their boathouse to lighten things up through the wetlands, but now we're fully loaded. Assuming the weather breaks tonight, we'll push off first thing in the morning.

Bemidji's been great to us, but we've got to get out of here. It's too easy to get stuck in towns with their warm beds and unlimited food. Long-distance hikers call this "town suck," and it's tough to leave once you get caught in a town's gravity field.

What happens is that I'll spend an extra day goofing off instead of hiking. Everything will be going great in some backwoods pizza-and-beer fantasyland. Then, reality steps in. It'll usually be something stupid, like someone breaking the line at the grocery store, but it messes with the fantasy of the town being perfect. I'd rather leave before the magic wears off.

Onward south, to the Gulf

Making miles

TWELVE HOURS LATER

Good god, we overdid it today. I stayed up all night writing a newspaper article, packing, repacking, and flipping out about everything. You know, the usual. I almost fell asleep in the stern, so we switched places for a while. I have no clue how long I slept in the bow, but I'm glad Jess is a total badass and paddled us solo while weaving through Wolf Lake and Lake Andrusia. We finally stopped on Starr Island and watched the sun set over the glassy water.

I know this part of the trip is coming, and I hate it. I'm getting super-antsy about our schedule, money, weather, etc. I can't shake this feeling. It's pointless and stupid, and I'm a total sucker for it.

I put myself through this same mental torture for months when I thru-hiked the Appalachian Trail. "Let's see. Thanksgiving divided by some completely unrealistic miles per day equals..."

Madness. Pure madness. This time, I do hereby resolve to chill the hell out.

(Narrator's Note—John did not, in fact, chill the hell out on this journey.)

Harold, the digital voice on the weather radio, predicts wild weather for the next few days. Thanks, Harold. It's blowing 10 miles an hour right now, and the forecast calls for 25 MPH or more with stronger gusts. Thunderstorms too. You know, "Fun."

The peepers (frogs) are loud and active tonight. They're feasting on the hordes of mosquitoes all around. We're inside the tent, and there are—I swear we counted—47 enormous blood-sucking mosquitoes desperately trying to get through the tent mesh to feed on our warm, succulent bodies. After we go into the tent, we kill any mosquitoes that follow us in. Bastards. The tent looks like a horror movie set from the bloodstains left on the walls. Mosquitoes suck.

Get it?
Mosquitoes suck.
I should get some sleep.
Yes, sleep would be good.
Zzzzzzzzzz

May 19, 2005

LAKE WINNIBIGOSHISH
MILE 116

Nicknamed "Lake Winnie" by the locals, Lake Winnibigoshish is Minnesota's third biggest lake. Translated from Ojibwe, Winnibigoshish means "dirty water," from how the lake rocks and rolls when the wind picks up. This wave action can be severe, and boaters often get into trouble when caught in bad weather.

Winnibigoshish can also mean "Damn, that's a big lake!" It's about twelve miles across as the crow flies, and one of the biggest obstacles in this stretch of the Mississippi. Technically, it's the widest part of the entire Mississippi River.

Back home two weeks and 1,600 miles away, we planned to get up before dawn and paddle straight across during the calmest part of the day. Heavy wind and cold waves smacked us back to reality. We tried to skirt the shoreline, but the waves spat us back after 100 yards. We headed back to shore until the wind calmed down.

After a couple of hours, we set out for a white-knuckle day of paddling. The wind was in our faces the entire time, making those seventeen miles around the lake the most challenging part of the trip so far. I thought we were in over our heads more than a few times.

The bow came down hard every time we went over a big wave. There was no time to eat or sneak a drink of water. We were both getting colder, weaker, hungrier, and thirstier. Not even sure if 'thirstier' is a word, but that's what we were.

After several hours of this "fun," we were getting surly with each other. I mean, screaming always helps, right? It wasn't pretty, and I'll be damned if I want every day to be like this.

Things improved when we reached the other side of the lake. We met a group of North Dakotans who wanted to share their dinner with us. It's been my experience that it's best not to argue with a 74-year-old North Dakotan priest, so we ate fresh-caught walleye with all the fixings. A dessert of ibuprofen (nicknamed *I-be-boatin'*) and the day was complete. Thank you, kind souls.

Today was our hardest and scariest yet, and I'm hoping things chill out for a while.

Onward

May 20, 2005

TWENTY YEARS LATER

First off, we actually really like cold-weather paddling. No crowds! No bugs! It's fun if you have the right gear and attitude for it. We had the attitude, but not proper cold-weather gear for those first few weeks. I'd hoped we'd luck out and get calm weather for the crossing, but that wasn't in the cards.

We were still figuring out how to paddle together. To keep a canoe going straight, paddlers usually stay on opposite sides. The bow (front) paddler sets the pace, and the stern (back) paddler calls when to switch. Jess is the better paddler, and early on, I wasn't all that confident in my own skills. There's a weird power dynamic when one person's giving the commands, and I had to get over it. Skirting Winnie in sketchy conditions beat that into me fast.

We weren't that far from shore, but the wind and waves were a frothy mess. Nobody else was out there, and for good reason. It was early in the season, the water was frigid, and the thought of getting tossed out of the boat, climbing back in, bailing it out, and limping to shore? Yeah. No, thank you.

Then add trying to pitch a tent and start a fire with frozen hands and a body shutting down. That wouldn't just make for a bad day. It could have been a *really* bad one.

COHASSET, MINNESOTA
MILE 158

We stopped in Cohasset for laundry, lunch, and, most importantly, hot showers. The truck stop showers cost $3 and were worth every penny. Our first hot showers in over a week were sorely needed.

Every scrap of gear is spread out on the dock, soaking up the sun. It's rained almost every day thus far, so everything stays damp. Not necessarily wet, but definitely damp, and definitely *funky*.

The river rarely flows in one direction for very long up here. Our record is about six miles in a straight line. The Mississippi flows north-ish for the first sixty miles, then cuts back to the southeast toward the Gulf of Mexico. Hairpin turns regularly mean that no matter what, the wind will soon be in your face.

Wind and mosquitoes were the words for this week. Their effects are interwoven; we've dealt with them individually and as the product of an unholy union.

The wind has been our constant companion, mostly blowing kisses in our faces. We've had sustained winds for several days, making things challenging. By challenging, I mean "opportunity for success," and by "opportunity for success," I mean "extra workout today. No charge!" It still beats being back in the office.

Pelicans taking flight

The mosquitoes have come out with a vengeance. I have a strong distaste for mosquitoes, but unfortunately, they've acquired a taste for me. It's fine as long as we're on the water, but once we hit the shore, they're coming for blood. I often end up in the corner of the tent, rocking myself to sleep in a fetal position and muttering something about B-52s attacking. I have no idea how Jess puts up with me.

I'm convinced the state of Minnesota has a covert mosquito training facility back in the hinterlands. As cold as the weather's been, it doesn't seem to bother the damn mosquitoes. I bet little old Lutheran ladies are cooking up hotdishes and holding sewing circles to knit tiny wool sweaters for the buggers so they can get a jump on the season. It pays to be hardy up here.

BUTT INERTIA

Look. I'm a slothful individual. I can heat a house with burnt time. I was born on December 31st and arrived just under the tax deduction wire for the year. Odds are I'll be late to my own funeral. You get the idea.

That said, I think the only way to achieve anything is to just get off your butt and start. Set a goal and move toward it. The details will work themselves out. Don't sweat the small stuff. Any progress is good progress. Just do something. Anything.

Tell people what your plans are. Parents, family, friends, your dog, strangers off the street—whoever. Some will be supportive. Some will say you're an idiot. Listen to the former, but don't ignore the latter. It helps to have people to face up to when you're scared out of your wits and want to quit. Peer pressure isn't always bad.

Taking the chance of falling on your face is good for you. When I'm old and grayer, I don't want to regret not trying something just because I was lazy or doing busy work. Life's far too short for that. My dad worked himself into the grave when I was still young, and I doubt he would've asked for more time at the office if given the choice. This trip down the Mississippi River is one of the hardest things I've done—but also the most fulfilling.

I was a train wreck in the months leading up to the trip. Sleepless nights spent obsessing over details, worrying about failure, and second-guessing the whole thing. But everything started falling into place the second the canoe hit the water. And of all the miles, that first one was the sweetest. I didn't know if we'll finish, but dammit, we're going to try.

I made a deal with myself at the end of my thru-hike: every five years, I'd do something cool. Hike the Pacific Crest Trail. Bike across the country. Build a house from scratch. Fly to the moon, whatever. Anything to get off my butt and live a little. If nothing else, I'd have some good stories to tell my (future) kids.

The first and hardest thing is to get off the couch and start. Once that butt inertia gets going, there's no stopping it.

May 23, 2005

ODE TO A MOSQUITO

Mosquito. Oh you @!*^%*# mosquito!
My loathing toward you knows no bounds.
None.
You are my nemesis.

No friend would torment me so.
Proboscis of pain. Poking. Probing.
Suck, suck, sucking away at me.
There will be no quarter for you.

Why must you torment me?
I've done you no harm, yet.
Come hither, my pretty. Closer. Closer.
Steady now. Steady.

So small. So, so small.
Time for you to meet your maker.
Leave me be.
Homme contre moustique.

GRAND RAPIDS, MINNESOTA

MILE 163

The state of Minnesota is now on the *"Cool Places to Visit but Too Cold for Me to Live"* list. The scenery, terrain, and people have all been outstanding. The winters must be brutal, but the folks we've met are the true embodiment of "cold hands, warm hearts."

In about an hour, we will tackle the longest portage of the trip. It'll be about 1,200 yards (you know, ¾ of a mile) of fun lugging our canoe and all our gear, and my back is already aching just thinking about it. After that, we'll have about a hundred miles with no dams, so the river should be flowing well. The sun is out and the birds are singing. It's a beautiful day.

Life is so damn good.

May 24, 2005

~

THE GLORY WORK OF PORTAGING

Thwarts are horizontal bars that go across the hull and connect the top edges of the canoe (gunnels.) These are typically pieces of hardwood, which add strength and rigidity to the craft. Many canoes have a special thwart in the middle called a yoke that has a built-in curve for your neck. You "put on the yoke" by flipping the canoe over and balancing it on your shoulders. It makes me feel like a plow horse heading out to plow the back forty acres.

Portaging through a cornfield

There's no way to get every little bit of sand, mud, and water out of the boat, so I'd get showered in all kinds of muck when I flipped it onto my shoulders. Sometimes I'd think I'd dodged the filth only to have a stream of nasty, muddy water run right down my back. There's nothing you can do about it besides cuss and get over it. That gear ain't gonna move itself.

There are 14 dams north of Minneapolis and 29 locks and dams south of it. In the headwaters stretch between Lake Itasca and Bemidji, we hauled around beaver dams and fallen trees about a dozen times. Portaging comes with the territory. It's part of the adventure, and it builds character.

So, so much character.

ANOTHER TOP TEN LIST

1. Watching a heron pluck a fish out of the water.
2. We listened to 400 pelicans take off as we floated by. They sounded like a bunch of white-feathered helicopters.
3. Paddling with a great tailwind on Lake Winnibigoshish for a bit. Nothing like being scared silly while making good time.
4. Full moons, new moons, and every moon in between.
5. Being stared at by bald eagles.
6. Watching a porcupine wander around camp, trying not to stick itself.
7. Thinking. Thinking. More thinking.
8. Listening to the red-winged blackbirds serenade us.
9. Watching the loons dive under the canoe and pop up twenty yards away.
10. Meeting some great people. Real salt-of-the-earth folks.

FORESTRY STATION BAR AND GRILL
JACOBSON, MINNESOTA - MILE 206

Roses are wet.
Violets are wet.
Everything is wet.
Please stop raining.

The weather has been consistent if nothing else. It's rained fifteen of the last nineteen days, and the forecast calls for more of the same. Hard rain. Soft rain. Misty rain. Foggy rain. *All* the rains.

Yesterday, it started raining just as we woke up, so we packed up a wet tent and damp gear, again. The wind was blowing, and temperatures were in the low forties—perfect conditions for hypothermia. This icy rain creeps into every nook and cranny and chills you to the bone.

After a couple hours of paddling, my rain pants started to leak. No, not just leak: this was a spectacular, complete, utterly miserable failure. A waterproof-breathable thong would have been about as useful and way more sassy.

Jess asked how I was doing, and I mumbled some bullshit about being fine. Fifteen minutes later, I was wrapping our tent's ground cloth around me like a kilt to stay warm.

Both of us were getting cold and needed some dry clothes and hot coffee, STAT. We were watching out for each other, and nothing was critical, but we needed to deal with being wet and turning blue by the minute.

After a few hours, we arrived at the bridge where Jacobson, MN (pop. 150), was *supposed* to be. We planned to hike to town, change clothes, and drink all the coffee in Minnesota. Instead, all we saw was a concrete outhouse.

Shit.

We ran to the outhouse to escape the weather. It was no palace, but at least it was dry. After a while, we decided to look for our missing town. If that didn't work out, we'd head back to the outhouse and cook some food—any port in a storm and all that.

We headed up the road and soon saw a homemade sign for the Forestry Station Bar and Grill. Okay, this looked promising.

A mosquito bit me right in the middle of my forehead. Minnesota is the only place where you can get a mosquito bite while drifting into the icy embrace of hypothermia.

We made it, slinking in like a couple of wet cats. The place looked like an old American Legion Hall—bare concrete floor, a bar on one side, folding tables and chairs on the other. An ancient video game buzzed and blinked in the corner. A total dive.

I was in love.

It was about noon, and Norm, the bar's owner, was chatting with some of the early arrivals. We ordered burgers, and he fired up the coffeemaker. I needed a beer, as it had already been a long day, and one must stay hydrated for medicinal purposes.

The wind howled as the rain fell in sheets. The TV weather guy predicted more storms overnight. Things weren't looking good for staying dry.

After another burger and beer, Norm started talking us into spending the night in his camper out back. Another hour passed, and the rain kept pouring. The bottle of Mad Dog 20/20 behind the bar gave me a come-hither look. The weather guy looked downright giddy to finally get a forecast right.

Forestry Station Bar and Grill, Jacobson, MN

We gave in and said we'd stay. Norm and I went to get the canoe and gear. It was so muddy that his son had to drag it out with his four-wheeler.

A steady stream of locals found their way onto the cracked black vinyl barstools. Carpenters, loggers, builders, and even an ex-canoe racer came in for beers and gave us some pointers. Folks would leave and be replaced ten minutes later like clockwork. A few guys came by for a second shift to talk about the trip and trade lies.

Jess went with Norm's wife, Sandy, to catch the finale of *American Idol* while I held down the fort watching *Dawn of the Dead*. Sandy also insisted on throwing our wet clothes into the dryer. Our tab for the night? Seven dollars.

Over the years, that camper had been home to deer hunters, snowmobilers, and other paddlers who had found themselves sucked into the Forestry Station vortex. We slept like babies.

After breakfast, Norm took us back to the river. We've seen some fantastic sights, but people like Norm and Sandy make the trip. When things start to go sideways, we seem to meet a stranger who sets the world right again. Those moments give me back some faith in humanity. Now *THAT's* the real stuff.

I wouldn't trade it for anything.

May 26, 2005

Home Sweet Camper

LESSONS FROM A SKINNY EGRET

We saw a skinny white egret trying to catch his lunch today. He was tucked into a small cut next to the river, maybe thirty feet long and ten feet wide.

He spent most of his time squawking, flapping his wings, stamping his feet, chasing fish, and jabbing his beak into the water over and over again. I guess he was trying to herd the fish to the edge of the water, but it didn't appear to be working very well.

No luck. He was a scrawny little thing, and I hope his technique improves with time.

Blue herons, on the other hand, are all about patience. They step back, watch, and slowly work their way into position. Then, with one clean strike, lunch is served. Calm. Efficient.

Flailing around might look productive, but it doesn't get you anywhere.

Be more like the blue heron.

PALISADE, MINNESOTA, MILE 257

We're polishing off the last of three desserts at the Palisade Cafe here in lovely Palisade, MN (pop. 118). Nothing like a breakfast of rhubarb pie, chocolate cake, and hot pecan pie to get our motors running again. All were homemade, and all were delicious. No sweet tea yet, but I can't complain. We're still at least 600 miles north of the sweet tea line.

Palisade was a hopping river town back in the day. I love thinking about what it must have been like back then with the steamboats, boomtowns, roustabouts, floozies, and whiskey. Everybody knows you can't have a boomtown without floozies and whiskey.

Everyone here is having a garage sale today. We passed four sales on the half-mile walk from the river. Someone tried to convince us to buy a small table, but we had to decline the offer. Sweet table, though. Shame it wouldn't fit in the canoe.

May 27, 2005

Palisade, Minnesota. Population 118

~

AITKIN, MINNESOTA, MILE 288

We're easing into the day with a cup of coffee in the Rippling Waters Motel and RV Park lobby. Our room cost seventy bucks, but it's the first place we've paid for since Cohasset. We can't afford to do this often, but we're willing to splurge now and then for a soft bed and a hot shower. We're both feeling under the weather and need to take it easy for a bit.

Our room looks like a bomb went off in it. Gear and clothes are draped over every doorknob, hanger, and lampshade. The tent and rainfly are stretched from one end of the room to the other so they can air out. It's nice to have everything dry for once, but it smells like a wet dog in here now.

Aitkin is a neat little town of about 2,000 folks. Like many towns around here, Aitkin grew out of an influx of German, Norwegian, French, and Swiss workers during the mid-1800s logging boom. Descendants of those early immigrants still live in the area and share many common last names.

The only stoplight in the county is in downtown Aitkin, at the intersection of MN 210 and Minnesota Avenue. They're pretty proud of it. All directions start with, "Go to the light, then head…" It reminds me of my hometown of Climax, NC. Our stoplight is right up the road from the Tank and Tummy and the Climax General Store. They're pretty proud of that light, too.

We bought supplies at Paulsen's Grocery. Paulsen's has been in the same family for over fifty-five years. They still wear green aprons, and real baggers still take your groceries to your car. That's real service, and a far cry from the ring-it-up-yourself, pay-in-the-slot, carry-it-to-your-car model that's become the norm. I didn't have a car, but I still tipped the guy.

We went to the Beanery coffeehouse to get caffeinated and check email. Before the trip, I wanted to get as far away from the outside world's garbage as possible. If something big happens, we'll hear about it eventually. I couldn't care less about the tripe that passes for news these days anyway. Celebrity drama, shady political dealings, and talent show runner-ups don't mean much right now.

I asked the kids working at the Beanery what there was to do in Aitkin on a Saturday night.

"Dude, you're looking at it."

We saw a lot of opportunistic lawn mowing today. Because of all the rain, they have to hack down the jungle whenever they can. It's still overcast and chilly, but grass waits for no one. You've got to go slow on the riding lawn mowers lest you hydroplane in the puddles. Minnesotans seem pretty adept at this, and I haven't heard of any drownings by mower, yet.

Jess and I have gotten along fine for the most part, considering we spend most of our time within eight feet of each other. If we can get through this trip, we can get through anything.

We're both feeling a bit ragged. It's been tough to relax with the rain and the chilly weather. We're a few days ahead of schedule, so we'll take our time getting out of town this afternoon. I have to remind myself this isn't a race to the Gulf of Mexico. It's easy to get wrapped up in where we are now, comparing it to some wild guess I plugged into a spreadsheet months ago back home, a place that now feels like a million miles away.

We'll get there when we get there.

May 29, 2005

BAXTER CANOE CAMPSITE, MILE 336

What a great morning. The sun is shining, the birds are singing, and mosquitoes aren't eating me alive even though I'm shirtless. The glare from my porcelain-white skin must be blinding them. Today's going to kick all the butts.

We paddled thirty-eight miles yesterday to get to this little slice of heaven. We hadn't planned to go that far—it just kind of happened. The canoe seems to fly down the river by itself when things click like that. We'll take those easy miles whenever we can.

Yesterday, we planned to camp north of Brainerd, then stop in town first thing this morning. The first fifteen miles went quickly, putting Brainerd easily within reach. The map showed a campsite on an island right next to the town. When we got there, that island was under a foot of water. No big deal—the noise from town was too loud anyway. We decided to push on because we were making such good time.

We stopped around 9 p.m., with just enough time to set up the tent before it got dark. What a great, long day. Although my sore muscles say otherwise, I still can't believe we're way up here doing the thing.

Each day has been an adventure with new things to see and new people to meet. Every minute is filled with living instead of coasting through like in the "real world." It doesn't get any more real than this. I feel like every fiber of my being has finally woken up after a long nap.

May 31, 2005

LITTLE FALLS, MINNESOTA, MILE 380

Just had a great breakfast at the Black and White Café. The Black and White is a funky place, serving as a diner, bookstore, and local hangout. It's got an Art Deco vibe that reminds me of downtown Asheville, NC. You can tell the owner has put his heart into the place.

We (*ok, me, whatever*) were craving biscuits in the worst way, and they came through in spades—two biscuits, sausage gravy, hash browns, and orange juice. If these guys delivered, I'd call for a breakfast airdrop every morning.

This week has been amazing. Cold rain, bright sunshine, and everything in between. The river is changing character. Just a week ago, it was less than one hundred feet wide. It's not uncommon for it to be a half-mile across now.

The mosquitoes are out in force. You can hear them getting louder when the sun starts to set. Mosquitoes are crepuscular, meaning they're most active at dusk and dawn. They're not so bad during the day, but a nightmare once the sun goes down. After we zip up the tent for the night, there's no coming out until morning.

We're seeing more man-made development. Homes, dams, towns, and factories are regular sights now. Two weeks ago, we fell asleep to the music of the loons. Last night, we dozed off to the lullaby of a riding lawnmower.

With all the rain, the river is running faster, making it easier to cover our miles. The wind is something we constantly have to contend with though. If it's not in our faces, we'll paddle about four miles per hour at a moderate pace. With a strong headwind, we practically stall if not for a furious effort. No slacking allowed.

Cooking in the wind has been "interesting." Our one-burner propane stove puts up a valiant fight, but it's useless without a wind shield. The best trick we've found is wrapping a sleeping pad around it, though not too close, since a canister explosion would get all shrapnelly and leave us with one hell of a pasta mess to clean up.

Cooking in the wind

YESTERDAY WAS SUPPOSED to be an easy 25-mile day. If things went well, we'd maybe even sneak in a shower at Crow Wing State Park. It sounded like a great plan. The first ten miles were cake, but the last fifteen were just a pain for some reason. We just couldn't get in a groove. If not for the faster current, we'd probably still be paddling.

Holy hell—the water coming out of the dam at Little Falls was kicking all kinds of butt today. HUGE waves! The portage route was washed out, and there was a low bridge to deal with downstream. We lashed everything down, talked through our plan to run the route, and did the damn thing. Jess is great at reading rivers, and we got through with nary a drop getting into the canoe. Nice!

Little Falls Dam

Oh yeah, another lesson learned today. Never, ever, roll up and seal the drybags until you're absolutely ready to pack them in the canoe. I can't count the number of times I've had to reopen and reseal a dry bag to add one last thing. I mean sure, it's a First-World problem and all that, but it's beyond annoying.

Got some sun for the first time in days, so things are looking up. Sometimes we get confused when this big, bright, shiny thing pops out of the sky. Now I know what Punxsutawney Phil goes through when they drag him out of his hole every spring. Poor thing.

June 1, 2005

SKINNY DIPPING WITH A SNAPPING TURTLE

"Hi! My name is John, and I'm a skinny dipping addict."

If there's a swimming hole around, chances are I'm going in. Nothing else gets the blood moving like jumping into the water wearing nothing but your birthday suit.

Last night I went swimming *au naturel* for the first time since we got on the river. Until now, it's been too damn cold to even *think* about swimming. Maybe not if you're one of those folks who like Polar Bear Swims on New Year's Day, but I'm a total wuss. It's been a shame to skip these great swimming holes, but turning into a human icicle ain't in my vision.

After we set camp last night, I went for a stroll while Jess stayed back and wrote in her journal. While wandering around, I found a cool trail to the river, which unfortunately also passed through a healthy stand of stinging nettles.

I couldn't help myself. At first, I tiptoed through and tried to avoid them. That was a pointless enterprise, and soon I just plowed through and hoped for the best. Nettles or not, I was going for a swim.

They don't call them stinging nettles for nothing.

My arms and legs felt like they were on fire. There's not much you can do about nettle stings besides grin and bear it until the pain subsides. Right then, I was doing more bearing than grinning.

I spied a large tree that had fallen into the water. That was going to be my highway to the river. I took off my clothes and laid them on the trunk, carefully avoiding any more nettles in my now unguarded and quite vulnerable state. I'm sure Mom would be proud of her buck-naked son standing in the middle of a nettle patch.

I made my way to the tree trunk and climbed on. I was halfway down when a giant snapping turtle slid off the tree and flopped into the river. That wouldn't be so bad, except he splashed down right where I planned to get in.

Not good.

Not good at all.

My skin was burning red from the nettles as the mosquitoes turned my ass into an all-you-can-eat buffet. I had to make a decision and make it fast. Either hike back through the nettles and resume that slow torture, or get in the water to rinse off.

I eyeballed where the snapper plopped in and saw nothing but dark water flowing through the branches. All I could think of was that thing waiting to take a chunk out of my hide.

"Surely he swam off."

"He's going to bite me in the nether regions if I jump in."

"This isn't good."

"No, it's not."

"John, you're not the sharpest knife in the drawer, are you?"

"No. No, I am not. You already know that. Shut up."

I decided to take my chances. The mosquitoes were feasting on me, and I couldn't just sit there like a human sacrifice. Mustering up whatever courage I had left, I shimmied down the tree, making as much noise as possible. I took one last pitiful look at the shore, then jumped in. Here goes nothing.

Man, that water was cold! My chest felt like someone was sitting on it, and I couldn't catch my breath. Worse than anything was the thought of that turtle sizing me up for a snack.

I was feeling pretty skittish about the whole affair. Aside from possibly having appendages bitten off, I didn't want to explain to Jess why her idiot boyfriend was chasing a big turtle in the river in the first place. I doubt she'd be too surprised, but I really didn't want to have *that* conversation.

I swam away from the hidden turtle as fast as I could and started to warm up. The mosquitoes chewed on any part of me above water. I'd dive under to escape them, only to think about the turtle waiting for me. I bet he'd already called a bunch of his turtle buddies to come over for dinner.

I'd had enough. Turtle or not, I had to swim back, pull myself up the tree trunk, and get the hell out of there. Once out of the water, the mosquitoes tore into me with a vengeance. I grabbed my clothes and made a frantic run for the tent. I jumped inside, just in front of a swarm of the flying beasties.

"How was the swim?"

"Oh, fine. Very relaxing."

I forgot to mention the turtle.

June 5, 2005

GO WITH THE FLOW

If you pay close attention to the river, you can spot where the water moves fastest. It looks smoother on top than the surrounding water, almost like a big neon arrow that says *"PADDLE HERE."*

Out here, speed changes you'd never notice in a car are obvious. Moving five feet over into the current adds about half a mile per hour to our speed. The paddle blades feel like they're dipping into whipped cream instead of wet cement when we're in the sweet spot.

Staying in the flow gets you from point A to point B faster, even if the route looks longer. Cutting corners takes you out of the current and slows you down.

That's a life lesson I need to remember.

Before we launched, we had no idea how many miles we'd cover each day. We've never done a canoe trip this long, and there were a ton of variables to consider. Water depth, blowdowns, beaver dams, locks, motivation, illness, and who knows what else all affect our daily mileage.

Early on, we were lucky to make two miles per hour with all the twists and turns, low water, and mandatory oohing and aahing.

Now, we plan on about four miles per hour if the wind's not howling. It's just a matter of paddling until your muscles burn, and then paddling some more. The fastest so far was nearly six miles per hour while we were on Lake Winnibigoshish with a screaming tailwind. It got super sketchy, but what a ride!

SAUK RAPIDS SLALOM
SAUK RAPIDS, MINNESOTA, MILE 412

There aren't a whole lot of rapids to speak of on the Mississippi—maybe a half-dozen if the water's high. Well, the water's high right now, and the river just slapped our hands for being impatient.

Today was a long one. On top of paddling around forty miles, we portaged both the Blanchard and International Paper Company dams. The usual put-ins below the dams were underwater, so we had to carry everything farther downstream to a safer spot. I ended up carrying the canoe through a cornfield on the Blanchard Dam portage because it was easier than rock-hopping on the shore.

We were taking pictures of the dam from an old railroad trestle nearby when the floodgate alarms went off. *Gah.* Additional gates would be opening soon, and we had piled all our gear just a few inches above the waterline! We took off running down the hill, fearing that all our gear and canoe would be flushed downstream. Losing everything would have been a complete disaster, but Lady Luck was on our side and things worked out fine in the end. *(Note to self. Don't do that again.)*

Sauk Rapids are considered a Class I-II rapid in normal water levels. Rapids are classified from Class I to V, with Class I being the most benign and Class V being nearly unrunnable and extremely dangerous. With the water being up, I'd say it was a solid Class III, meaning there would be a fair amount of maneuvering involved, but it wouldn't be particularly dangerous if we flipped. Still, dumping here would be a total pain in the ass.

Sauk Rapids is just a half-hour from where we planned to spend the night. It was close to sunset, and we were tired from paddling and portaging all day. We hadn't been super careful securing everything after the last portage. We just tossed most of the gear in the canoe, except for a few things tied down. *Slackers.*

Our plan, as much as there was one, was to get near the rapid, pull over, and scout the river from the side. Barring that, we would hop from eddy to eddy and work downstream. Plan A went out the window quickly because there wasn't a good place to pull off with a view of the river. On to Plan B.

We could hear the water rushing in the distance but didn't see anything until we rounded the last bend. The river curves to the right, and we wanted to stay on the inside of the curve if possible. The safest place to be on an unknown river is on the inside of the curve—there's less current there and usually fewer hazards like fallen trees in the water.

The water quickly gained speed as we approached, and we were flying by the seat of our pants. The plan to duck behind an eddy was quickly scrapped due to the rushing water, not to mention our canoe wasn't made for that kind of maneuvering. This canoe is a go-straight-and-fast machine, not made to spin around at a moment's notice.

We made one last stab to sneak behind an eddy before diving into the teeth of the rapid. No luck. We'd have to run the rapids on the fly and hope for the best.

I looked down and thought of all the gear we would soon be fishing out of the water. It was close to sunset, the temperature was dropping, and we were both smoked from paddling all day. That was not going to be much fun.

Due to our limited mobility, we had to take the most direct route possible while still avoiding the bulk of the rocks. The canoe wasn't about to turn on a dime and change course, so we were committed whether we liked it or not. We made our way to the right, then back toward the middle. Rounding the bend, we knew we were in trouble. Waves crashed all around, and we were being funneled right where we didn't want to be.

Jess read the river like a boss, shouted directions over the roar of the water, and braced from the bow. She has a lot of control of the canoe from the bow and kept us off the worst of the rocks. My job was to provide the bulk of the steering to keep the canoe pointed downstream. Easier said than done with a canoe pushing six hundred pounds of gear and bodies.

The final obstacle was a massive rock in the middle of the river with a ledge just behind it. When there's a ledge like that, there's often a "keeper hole" where you can flip out but not get flushed downstream for a while. Great for playboating. Not so great with a loaded-down canoe.

The current pushed us sideways, and we were heading straight for the rock. This was going to be a close one.

With a huge effort and plenty of cussing, we muscled the canoe back on course. We hit the ledge and paddled with everything we had. One stroke, two strokes, one final flurry, and we were through! A few gallons of water came over the gunnels, but we didn't fall into the drink. Some days it's better to be more lucky than good.

We were pumped full of adrenaline after all that. My hands were shaking, and my body was numb. The final few hundred yards flew by as we paddled to the St. Cloud University dock and made our way to the tennis courts to camp.

Our arrangements to camp at St. Cloud U were another happy result of someone seeing the website and offering a place to stay for the night. There's no way we can stop everywhere, but it feels good knowing other folks are looking out for us.

We dodged a bullet today and will need to be more careful in the future. Impatience when the water gets bigger could end up being more than just a little hassle.

Onward, with caution.

June 2, 2005

KIDNAPPED IN MINNEAPOLIS
MINNEAPOLIS, MINNESOTA MILE 488

Funny thing, this kidnapping business. One minute you're paddling to Minneapolis, the next you're being whisked away for pizza, hot showers, and bedtime stories. We've received several offers out of the blue to crash in spare bedrooms, eat a home-cooked meal, and take a break from the river. We're touched by the offers and wish we could take everyone up on them. At that pace, it might take us a year to reach the Gulf. Would that be so bad? *Hmmm.*

Bill and his family were among the first folks to email us. At first, I hesitated to take him up on his offer because we were making great time. I'm going to forget all about that sort of stuff in the future, though—this was a great visit.

Bill and Laurie live outside Minneapolis with their kids, Jack and Kate. Bill is a prosecutor, and he used his persuasive talents to good effect. Here's the email he sent.

I received an email from friends of mine with the National Park Service/MNRRA about your adventure. I wish you all the best. My 8-year-old son proposed a canoe trip from Itasca to the Gulf about a year ago and we are in the initial stages of planning a trip from Itasca through the state of Minnesota (probably for next summer, if I will not kill myself doing it with him!). We will follow your trip with great interest -- and will read your journal entries for all the key insights.

If you need/want a warm place to spend the night, we've got a pretty nice guest room -- most importantly, it has its own bathroom with HOT shower.

In any event, if you have a chance to respond to this and know about when you will be in the Twin Cities, I am sure our children (Jack - 8, Kate - 6) would love to head down to the river to say hello and bring you some supplies, if needed."

Yeah, he played the Jack and Kate card.

We're both suckers for kids, so we had no choice but to visit. Turns out that Jack really wanted to paddle the river and knew his stuff about canoeing. It took Kate all of five minutes to adopt Jess. Hot showers, homemade pizza, and wonderful fellowship—it would take a lot to tear me out of this place.

We have long nylon straps with us for car-topping the canoe, but this was the first time they'd been used since we left Lake Itasca. It was unnerving to put the canoe on top of their minivan and then hit the freeway at 75 mph. That was weird, but nothing flew off on the short ride to their house.

Once back at their house, we tried to dry out our equipment in the few hours of sunshine before dark. It looked like an outdoor store exploded in their driveway, with bright nylon gear, paddles, and all our other damp stuff spread out all over the place. This gave us a good chance to get everything laid out and accounted for, and it was fun to show the kids how everything worked.

We love seeing kids get jazzed about doing things outside, and I expect we'll see Jack in National Geographic talking about a trip to some exotic locale soon. Kate was a doll and the best hostess we could ask for. It took a few minutes for her to warm up to this couple of smelly strangers, but she was soon showing us everything around the house.

After a night away, we were ready to get back on the river. It was time to go through the first of 29 locks between here and St. Louis. Goodbye to small lakes and hello to big barges. This is when Big Muddy will really start to live up to its name.

~

THE FIRST LOCKS - UPPER ST. ANTHONY'S FALLS

Before the trip, I was most afraid of locks, barges, and wing dams. I'd never seen a wing dam, and we don't have barges and locks back home either.

Upper St. Anthony's Falls Lock was the first lock we passed through. It just so happens to be the biggest on the entire river, with a fifty-foot drop from one level to the next.

We'd read up on the locking procedures but were still anxious about the whole thing. It's hard to get your head wrapped around paddling into a 600-foot concrete box, watching the massive doors shut behind you, having the water sucked from under you, then being lowered five stories down to the next level like a slow-motion elevator. I couldn't stop thinking about all that water behind those doors as we were lowered down.

"I know those doors have worked thousands of times, but what if they fail the one time that we're in here?"

The float buoy shrieked like a banshee against the concrete wall, completing the whole effect. Yeah, that was super relaxing.

Upper St. Anthony's Falls Lock

What was waiting for us when the doors creaked open? *Whirlpools? Giant octopus? Water Aliens from Mars?* We even had a line of visitors watching us from the bridge above. No pressure. Nope.

I'm not gonna lie. It was scary as hell.

But things went smoothly enough, and the Corps of Engineers

folks wished us well. One of them told us to have a drink for him at Pat O'Brien's in New Orleans. It never hurts to have a semi-arbitrary goal to work toward.

Minneapolis Grain Belt Beer Sign

I loved seeing Minneapolis and St. Paul from the river. Even the industrial areas. Hell, especially the industrial areas. It's a view that you don't get while driving past at 70 miles an hour. Rusted barges tied to the banks, abandoned docks, and collapsing buildings. I've always liked poking into abandoned barns and buildings ever since I was a kid. That's my jam.

One lock down, twenty-eight to go.

Onward South

Jess's Perspective

John has asked me to report on the "feminine perspective" of the Source to Sea Expedition. As a lady of the outdoors, I welcomed the challenge of broken nails and all. Eleanor Roosevelt said, "Do one thing every day that scares you". The day we paddled through Minneapolis personified that quote.

The city moved too fast compared with all of the other places we had been on this trip, and I didn't have lots of time to collect myself. Everybody said that the locks and dams were OK if you follow the rules (ask for lockage, enter lock, hold rope, wait for the horn to blast, exit lock). The experience of being locked through was something I feared. I thought it would be a rough ride because of the dangerous currents produced by the lock chamber drawing in or pushing out water.

As we paddled up to the first lock (Upper St. Anthony's Falls), I was trembling, literally trembling. I knew that we would eventually go through some 29 locks, but I wasn't sure it was safe, and I could see myself being pulled to the bottom of the river. As it turns out, the lock was relatively tame, slowly lowering us as if we were a toy boat floating in a bathtub just starting to drain. I was relieved, but it was still strange with the ominous lock walls slowly getting higher and higher. The closing and opening of the gigantic doors is slow and controlled, and I couldn't keep from humming the Darth Vader theme music...Dum dum dum dum da dum dum da dum.

In the definition of adventure, the outcome is unknown. In this adventure, for many days, we do not know the specifics of many things. Every day brings uncertainty and adventure. The only way to know is to do it. The experience makes us stronger, and that is why the famous First Lady dared us to do things that scare us.

I'll have to tell you about the nail breaking another time. For now, we are ready to continue our trip downstream. Bon Voyage!

PART TWO
MINNEAPOLIS TO ST. LOUIS

MELLOW MONDAY

Before we started, we guesstimated we'd have enough time between semesters to reach the Gulf of Mexico if we stayed on schedule. Being chained to this stupid schedule has me completely stressed out. I'm over it.

Today is Mellow Monday.

I'm not sure how far we'll get today. I don't care. Whatever it is, it's going to be mellow. I'm driving Jess nuts with all my freaking out about finishing. Considering we still have over a thousand miles to paddle, it's silly to worry about it now.

This trip is starting to feel like a job, so Mellow Monday is about relaxing and going with the flow. Today, we're eating, playing, and taking a break from this self-imposed pressure cooker. I should have taken this approach from Day One.

We got on the river about eight this morning and poked down-stream for a few hours. The barge traffic has been light, and we've seen few other boaters out. It's weird having the river to ourselves again after the weekend rush—just a few guys out fishing and that's about it. Kind of nice, to be honest.

We stopped for lunch just before Lock No. 3. A barge was waiting to go through, so we decided to bypass the lock and portage to a small lake parallel to the river. I'm not a big fan of portaging, but this one was easy peasy. *Nothing* is getting me riled up on Mellow Monday.

It was such a pretty area, so we decided to hang out and cook lunch instead of pressing on. Lunchtime turned into nap time—a very mellow thing to do. Paddling down the lake was great. The water was much clearer than the river, so you could see the fish swimming around. Too chilly for a swim, but just right for dangling toes in the water.

The sun is shining, the wind is calm, and the mosquitoes aren't feasting on us. I could get used to this.

Every day should be like Mellow Monday.

June 6, 2005

❧

RED WING, MINNESOTA, MILE 550

We've spent a day and a half here in Red Wing. The bluffs lining the river are absolutely beautiful! So chill to paddle through. Sarah, Jessica's buddy from her AmeriCorps NCCC years, has given us the run of her house. Sarah was once crowned Miss Red Wing. So yeah—we're staying with royalty. Everybody knows Sarah. Every. Damn. Body. She's the best.

Yesterday was our first complete day off in three weeks, and we were ready for a break. We picked up our mail and supplies from the post office, then bought groceries and a few other essentials. The day flew by quickly, and we're leaving this afternoon. The river is calling, and that river ain't gonna paddle itself.

Docking at the marina was pretty funny. We tied up at the end of a long string of yachts, sailboats, and houseboats. Most of those boats never leave the slip because they're too expensive to run. I could smell the jealousy in the air as we pulled in. Our muddy canoe doesn't cost a dime to run, other than copious amounts of food and water.

One of us is not like the other, Red Wing, MN

It's getting warmer, so we sent our cold-weather clothes and sleeping bag home. A five-dollar sheet and blanket from the thrift store will be our bed for the rest of the trip. We also sent home unused gear and anything we found better replacements for. Carrying less gear and clothes means less to keep clean, secure, maintained, and most importantly, dry.

I also replaced my goofy straw hat with the plastic green visor for something more practical. That hat reminded me of my grandfather. He'd wear one while driving his red-belly Ford tractor around the farm that his moonshine money paid for in the 1940s. The revenuers found out about it but couldn't track him down for a while.

They wised up and followed my grandmother when she hiked

through the woods to an abandoned house where my granddad hid. She'd put a ladder up to the second-story window and bring him food and water every day. Paw Paw ended up doing a couple of years of involuntary labor on the federal farm in Ohio.

He would always pile a bunch of us grandkids in the back of his blue Ford pickup and take us to the Julian Curb Market for Cokes and candy. He always paid with a big bill from his big black leather wallet. He loved kids, and I loved him. He was a good guy.

Contrary to earlier predictions, we haven't killed each other. Some people call canoes "Divorce Machines," but we've gotten along fine for the most part. Things are going well, we're in a groove, and every day brings something new.

The past week has flown by. We've gone through Grand Rapids, Prescott, Minneapolis, St. Paul, and Red Wing. We're also along the Wisconsin border for our second state.

Going through the Twin Cities was exciting and nerve-wracking due to the heavy boat traffic and numerous buildings along the river. We also went through the first five of the twenty-nine locks we'll see before St. Louis. The locks are a marvel of engineering, even when going through with white-knuckled grips on the paddles.

Media attention is starting to pick up now. Greta Cunningham from Minnesota Public Radio came in this morning to record a segment for *Morning Edition*. She was an absolute pro, and while we were doing the interview, I couldn't help but listen to her calm public radio voice. Back home, we're always listening to National Public Radio, and it was pretty cool getting featured on one of their syndicated programs.

Audubon Magazine also interviewed us for an article. It's been great helping get the word out about Audubon's Upper Mississippi Campaign, and I hope they're seeing some results from our expedition. Those folks are doing some good work protecting this resource and reconnecting people to the river.

Everything is getting bigger. The river, the cities, the barges. *Everything*. It's neat to paddle under a towering bridge and see cars driving overhead. Just a few weeks ago, we were squeezing under remote two-lane bridges back at the headwaters.

We paddle all day and rarely see anyone except for a few barges. One exception to this is being anywhere near a marina around quitting time on Friday. Any Friday. The zoo starts at 5:01 sharp, and it's every boat for themselves after that. Most folks don't go far from the boat ramps, though. I think there's an unwritten rule about taking your cabin cruiser more than three miles from the marina or something.

June 9, 2005

QUARTERS ONLY
LAKE CITY, MINNESOTA - MILE 614

Showers have been few and far between since we've been on the river. The last few weeks have been like paddling through a big refrigerator, and just cold enough to keep the stink down. Now it's heating up, and that heat begets a mighty funk and the need for more frequent showering.

Last night we camped at Hok-Si-La Municipal Park after a long day of paddling. We arrived after dark and soon had the tent up and gear stowed away. We then scouted the campground to see what it had to offer. I smelled like something the dog rolled in. It was grim, and the top of my wish list was a shower to get rid of the malodorous cloud surrounding me. Remember Pig Pen from the Charlie Brown shows? That was me.

Seriously. I reeked. Bad. Like, real bad.

After wandering around for a while, we found the shower house. I went back to grab my hygiene essentials—shampoo, soap, "miracle towel," and some clothes to change into. I also dug out my coin stash and went on the hunt to find a soda machine. I started this trip with a scorching caffeine addiction and needed a fix in the worst way.

This shower would be the longest, hottest, most excellent shower ever. A shower for the ages! Folks will write songs about how awesome this shower is. I ran back, giddy with the thought of washing off the dirt, mud, and sunscreen caked on me.

I burst into the shower house ready to scrub away. I probably needed to use a scouring pad on myself, but my little camp towel would have to do. It was late, and no one else was stirring about. All the better—more hot water for me.

I walked into the stall and scraped off my clothes. I had some crazy tan lines from wearing my PFD and sandals all day. My feet were criss-crossed with Z's, like they usually are ten months out of the year. Some of that tan was from the sun, but most of it was grime and destined to go down the drain. *Destiny,* I say.

The plan was to scrub myself down and wash my paddling clothes. They stank and needed serious attention. Lacking a Viking funeral pyre, a soak and stomp in the shower would have to do. Time for my clothes to face the suds.

I had maybe two tablespoons of shampoo left and just a dab of soap. A shower with Dr. Bronner's always makes me feel fresh, like a big, tingly peppermint patty.

Just as I turned the handle, I saw something out of the corner of my eye. No, *Norman Bates* wasn't trying to slash me. Just a small sign on the wall.

"QUARTERS ONLY"

I panicked, then felt like a punch-drunk prizefighter on the back end of the twelfth round. Hoping for a miracle, I reread the sign.

"QUARTERS ONLY"

Damn.

I had to find some quarters, or my whole plan would go down

the drain. Things went flying everywhere as I ripped open my toiletry bag. Out popped two dimes and a nickel. An errant penny rolled under the sink. Finally, twinkling in the blue fluorescent light, there they were…two lonely quarters. I couldn't get my caffeine fix, but it didn't matter. Those quarters were needed for something far more critical.

This had to be a speedy operation of funk removal. I opened my shampoo and soap bottles and looked at my composting pile of paddling clothes. They'd have to wait. Everything was ready to go.

I slipped both quarters into the slot, and steaming water soon bounced off my grimy skin. I pondered the cryptic writings on the bottle of Dr. Bronner's as I slathered on the soap.

"Exceptions eternally?"
"Absolute none!"
"All One?!"

I lathered the shampoo furiously through my greasy hair. Rinsed, and repeated.

Soon, the soap was rinsed off, and I could just soak away the day's effort. I folded my six-foot-three-inch self under the shower head. Then, it happened.

Silence.

Nothing but the drip, drip, drip of the last drops of water dribbling out of the shower. I heard Jess singing through the wall. She must have slipped past my flank with her stash of quarters. No time for jealousy now. I was starting to freeze.

The makers of my "miracle towel" are full of it. "Absorbs 1000 times its weight" my ass. It just kind of spreads the water around before begrudgingly sopping up a few drops. The chill of the Minnesota night crept in as I dried off my goosebumps as fast as I could.

I soaked my clothes in the sink with the last few drops of soap.

The water changed from clear, to murky, to a dark shade of mud. At least my shorts were a different shade of grime.

I stumbled back to the tent, a man defeated.

A man defeated...*but clean.*

FLASH FLOODS AND CHEESE CURDS

FOUNTAIN CITY, WISCONSIN - MILE 627

Today looked to be a typical Saturday on the river. Lots of recreational boaters out, with lots of recreational beers in hand. I'm not a teetotaler by any stretch, but I wonder if a guy should be piloting a speedboat while pounding their way through the back end of a twelve-pack.

We were up and moving at dawn for a few hours of relative peace, but once the crowds came out, we were back to dodging boats and wallowing in their churned-up wakes. I guess it's only fair to share the river on the weekends—the rest of the week we have it to ourselves.

After a few hours, we took a break at Fountain City, Wisconsin. There was a small dock by the boat ramp, so we tied off the canoe and walked towards town to find some food. A railroad bridge was about twenty yards away from the ramp, and about thirty minutes later, that bridge would turn out to be our best friend.

We went out to search for ice cream and coordinate a time to meet with our buddy Randi, who was driving up from Iowa. This was the only place we'd had cell phone reception all day, and even that was pretty iffy.

We made our phone calls, bought 200 pounds of junk food at a gas station, and returned to the canoe for a picnic. As we walked down the street, the wind picked up, and the sky turned a dark, angry black.

Jess said, "This is gonna get interesting."

That was a bit of an understatement.

We made it to the bridge just as the deluge hit. The wind came roaring from the northwest while lightning crashed all around. It was raining so hard you couldn't see ten feet in front of you. Things started getting a little hairy under the bridge, so we decided to run for real shelter. As luck would have it, the closest place was a bar named Joe's Place.

Fountain City sits at the base of a large hill, and traffic came to a standstill as the floodwaters rushed down the main street. We ran into the bar and sheepishly dripped in their doorway. It felt like being back at the Forestry Station Bar and Grill. Why did these places keep popping up in the worst weather? Luck? Faith? Baccuvian intervention? Who knows? Who cares? At least we were out of the storm.

The bar was like a million others I'd been to. Pool table in the back, neon signs everywhere, and posters promising a good time with friends if you just bought the beer they were hawking. The usual suspects were holding things down.

After dripping for a few minutes, I started to worry about the canoe. The last thing we needed was to lose that thing. Not only would it end the trip, but we'd also lose a lot of expensive gear. Neither option was fun to think about, so it was back to the maelstrom for me.

As soon as I stepped outside, I knew I was in for a fun time. Not in a fun "ha ha" kind of way, but more like a fun "I can't believe I'm in the middle of this mess instead of nuzzling a beer inside the warm confines of the bar" kind of way. It was raining cats, dogs, frogs, and horses at this point, but there was *no way* I was going to let that canoe vanish.

There was already a foot of water in the street. I returned to the dock and found the canoe still intact, but it was quickly filling up with water. At least it hadn't come loose from its moorings.

The ramp was now underwater, so I hoped for the best and jumped for the dock. I untied the canoe's lines and pulled the boat back to shore. Then I piled the gear on the bank and tied the canoe to a chain-link fence. With everything secure, I could finally chill.

After all that, I needed food and refreshment. I slogged back up the hill as water continued to pour down the street. Eventually, I returned to the bar where Jess had already met some new friends.

I ordered a beer, for medicinal purposes.

The bar was sponsoring a drawing for some random prizes that day. We felt lucky and bought three tickets. First drawing, nothing. Second drawing, nothing. Last drawing, nothing. This wasn't our day.

I was getting hungry, and I saw some bowls containing a white, blobby substance at the end of the bar.

Not pretzels.

Not peanuts.

Not popcorn.

Cheese curds.

Instead of the typical bar food down south, the good folks of Fountain City served their patrons bowls of raw white cheese curds. Cheese curds! What. The. Hell. Is. This. Madness?

Today I learned how much Wisconsinites are freaking nuts about their cheese products, no matter the shape, form, or stage of completion. People dipped their fingers in to grab globs of the curdled blobs dripping with cheese juice. I thought about eating a few, but the thought of multiple fingers mixed with milk products got in the way. I'm no culture snob, but that's too many appendages in that culture for me. Maybe next time.

After things calmed down, we paid our tab and headed back. Boaters were pulling up to the dock, drenched from the storm. We loaded the canoe, turned downstream, and thanked our lucky stars for another place to hide from the elements.

Viva Joe's Place! ¡Es un lugar de maravillas!

June 11, 2005

~

WEEKEND WARRIORS

Boats of all ages and states of repair descend on the water to swarm the river every weekend. Well-heeled captains of cabin cruisers are forced to share the water with teenagers on jet skis. Overloaded speedboats fly by, and fishermen sneak off to their favorite fishing holes. Any boat with enough horsepower will be dragging water-skiers and wakeboarders behind. It's always chaotic, but the sheer stupidity on the water today took things to a new level.

We stay close to the shore and out of the channel on the weekends. The upside to paddling near shore is that we're less likely to get run over, and that's a good thing. Big fan of not getting run over.

The downside is that we're out of the current and have to paddle harder to cover the same distance. They say you give a little to get a little, but it doesn't make getting down the river any easier.

We're usually on the water early and have the river for ourselves for a few hours before things get wacky. We'll see a few people fishing, but that's about it until noon. After that, it's every man, woman, and kid for themselves, and we just make the best of it.

Barge traffic tapers off on the weekends, but things get interesting for everyone when they come up the river. I'm sure barge captains look forward to the weekends as much as we do. Steering a 20,000-ton vessel through a bunch of water skiers, personal watercraft, and cabin cruisers in full-on party mode has got to be annoying.

Barges throw massive wakes in all directions. It's common to see them send eight-foot-tall wakes rolling behind. Some brave *(foolish?)* souls use these as jumps for their aquatic playground.

So we're just paddling along, watching as this madness goes down. A barge tow is coming upstream through the navigation channel. Nothing unusual. That's what they do. Boats are everywhere, pulling skiers and having a great time. It's getting crowded, but nothing unusual for a sunny Saturday afternoon.

Suddenly, a speedboat zooms past the barge, pulling three kids on an inflatable raft. Daddy's driving, and Mom's in the back, waving to the kids hanging on for dear life. They don't know how close they'd get today.

Daddy whips around in the middle of the navigation channel for one last pass while other boats dodge them. Kids screaming. Mom waving. Daddy chugging.

Charging back toward the barge, Daddy gets within twenty yards of the barge and pulls away at the last second. The kids held on and didn't fall off. I'm shocked we didn't have to pull them out of the water after that stunt.

"You're going to kill those kids!" the barge captain shouted from his loudspeaker.

Bad Daddy.

We spent the rest of the day dodging boats until dusk. After that circus, I was ready for the weekend to be over. Never thought I'd be so happy to see Monday.

We'd often see the same people over and over again. Boats would fly past us, then congregate on a beach. In a few hours, we'd paddle past their beach hangout. The herd of boats would pass us again on their way back to the marina.

One day, we met a group of boats led by a guy we'll call Joe. Joe stood out from the crowd. His sunburned, Rubenesque figure was crammed into an undersized personal watercraft, thinning hair waving in the breeze as he zigzagged through boat traffic like a man on a mission.

Joe wasn't too familiar with the protocol for locking through. Jess and I snuggled up next to the lock wall like usual when Joe and a couple of his companions came by in their overloaded craft. They had to move away when the lock door opened because they were well past where they should've been. After we locked through, Joe and company roared off in a show of underpowered hubris.

Rock on, Joe. You magnificent beast.

~

ANOTHER POOL CROSSING THIS MORNING. There are usually a few miles of flat water before we reach each lock and dam. Sometimes we can get away with paddling straight across the pool instead of skirting the shore, but it's a risk. We're completely exposed to the waves and weather once we're into a crossing. When the wind picks up, the waves aren't far behind.

Now and then, we catch a tailwind and make good time. Most of the time, the wind is straight in our faces. There's an upside to this. We can paddle directly into the waves without water coming over the gunnels.

The bow gets way up in the air when the waves are rocking. A canoe is most stable when both paddles are in the water, and paddles up in the air are useless. I'm digging in the stern while Jess is up front going over a wave. When she's paddling in the trough, I'm bracing off the back of the previous wave. We're a team, always. For some reason, it helps to curse a lot. The louder, the better. Trust me. It's *science.*

Jess said I kept her up all last night with my snoring. I don't doubt that, and I feel terrible about it. She's not getting the rest she needs, and it's not fair at all. Good sleep is a valued commodity out here. Every day I wake without a shiv in my neck is a good day. I wouldn't blame her.

So we got into a huge fight this afternoon. I asked Jess what we should do for our next long trip, and it started a discussion about finishing this trip before planning another one. Didn't help that I felt like crap and had been a snarky asshole all day.

That stirred up a bunch of other stuff we'd been holding in, and screaming at each other was a terrible way to spend an hour. I guess it's good to blow out the pipes and air out the junk now and then, but damn if it doesn't suck at the time. We cooled off eventually, like we always do. Paddling close to each other for ten hours a day makes ignoring each other *impossible.*

I have the attention span of a squirrel on a Mountain Dew and Pop-Rocks bender, and my brain's usually ping-ponging all over the place. There's always a song in my head, and I might be thinking about roof angles, pizza recipes, or something while talking about something entirely different. Most of the time, what comes out of my mouth is *technically* connected to the conversation, but those connections get pretty tenuous.

But I digress.

I felt a huge weight come off my shoulders once we got on the river last month. Whether we made it two miles or two thousand was secondary. Now that we're in the middle of this thing, I get to start thinking about what comes next. Canoe the Missouri? Bike cross-country? Another long trail? Who knows, but it's fun for me to think about. If nothing else, it takes my mind off the heavier stuff hanging over me.

I'm not entirely sure the current career path I'm barreling down in higher education will be for me. I've had some serious second thoughts about it for the past few months. I love to teach, and I'm a decent public speaker, but I struggle with the administrative side of it. Grading, paperwork, and class logistics aren't my strengths. The *"publish or perish"* hazing mentality in academia seems like spending the summer in Hell.

FOOD

CUISINE EN CANOË

Camping catalogs often feature Dutch ovens overflowing with cobbler and stew. That idyllic riverside feast is not our reality. Sure, if you're on a float trip with rafts loaded with coolers and goofy-named microbrews, the menu is amazing, but that's not our thing.

Those trips aren't about making miles. You spend half the time cooking and drinking instead of paddling. We both get bored silly sitting around a campsite and would rather be on the river than babysit some damn risotto.

Our cooking style consists of simple meals that are easy to prepare. We rarely cook breakfast, preferring to eat in the canoe while we're on the water. We've settled into this routine for several reasons: cold in the beginning, mosquitoes later on, and scorching heat now.

We store our food in 5-gallon buckets with special screw-off lids and stow them directly behind Jess's seat. About an hour in, she spins around and digs out whatever looks good for breakfast. Some days it's a peanut butter and jelly sandwich, other days it's crackers and cheese.

She adds flair and panache to her creations—stuff I can't even begin to replicate. Twizzlers tied in knots for garnish, for example. Once she's done creating, I reach up with my paddle like a pizza server and get my share.

If Julia Child had a smokin' hot PFD tan line and filleted Oreos for snacks, she'd be Jess.

We usually stop early in the afternoon to cook dinner, chill, and then press on for a few more hours. This has several advantages—we both sleep better, the last few hours of paddling fly by, and we don't have that bonked-out feeling we used to get from waiting till the end of the day to eat a big meal.

Back on the Appalachian Trail, I lived off mashed potatoes, Fritos, Little Debbies, and oatmeal. I still gag at the sight of instant oats. I basically ate like a trash panda. This time, we've tried to eat better. Jess wasn't having that nonsense, and I don't blame her.

One of the benefits of a canoe trip is the ability to carry more and better food. It's not just about quantity, but variety and freshness. You're limited to how much you can carry when you're backpacking. Carry too much, and your pack weighs a ton. Carry too little, and you starve. The canoe allows us to carry fresh food, as well as canned goods, if we want. Three buckets of food are overkill, but we've never run out.

We didn't bring a cooler. One less thing to portage, and I never have to chase down ice at some random gas station. No regrets whatsoever.

Sloth has its virtues.

THE OLD RELIABLE - WORLD'S EASIEST ONE-POT MEAL

(serves two)

This is our go-to meal. It's the first thing I ever cooked for Jess. We've probably eaten it a million times, and it's on the menu for every trip. Eyeball measurements are fine. Most of the time, I'm lucky if I can find my spoon, much less measure anything.

- 12 ounces of pasta (any kind, we like the tri-colored twist type)
- 4 ounces or so of Italian dressing (about half a small bottle)
- 3 ounces of cheese (whatever you have. We use cheddar and parmesan)
- 1 small onion
- 3-4 carrots, chopped
- 1 small can of pineapple chunks
- Salt and pepper to taste
- Whatever else you want to throw in (nuts, spices, garlic, chicken, etc.)

In a 2-liter or larger pot, bring the pasta to a boil and cook until tender. Don't overcook, and make sure it doesn't boil over. Drain the pasta and return it to the pot. *(Hint: cut the bottom four inches off a gallon milk jug and stab some holes into the bottom. Voilà! Instant strainer.)*

Dice up the cheese, onion, and carrots, and dump them in. Open the can of pineapple, drink the juice, then dump in. Add whatever else you have on hand. Stir in the Italian dressing.

Eat until you see the bottom of the pot.

Enjoy the sunset.

Dinner for Two

MUSINGS
GEAR, YURTS, AND OVERTHINKING

ON GEAR: KEEP IT SIMPLE

We're big believers in keeping things simple on a trip. First and foremost: take the least amount of gear necessary. Right away, you've cut out half the hassle—less to keep dry, secure, or clean. We'll still bring a few luxury items, but having some discipline helps us make more miles when we want to. More importantly, carrying less weight means less fatigue and less stress on your body.

I'm not an ascetic. I'm just a lazy, slothful human who loves being outside.

It took us a while to dial in the right mix, but our gear now works for us. It fits our style and our needs. Most of it pulls double duty, and the few things that don't serve that one purpose really well.

All of this circles back to that slothfulness. For instance, I don't use a self-inflating pad. I'd rather toss my foam pad on the ground and nap anywhere without worrying about leaks or hauling around a patch kit. Cheap, durable, lightweight, and comfortable-ish. What's not to like?

YURT YEARNINGS

While we were organizing this trip, I came across some of my Appalachian Trail (AT) journals. I'd forgotten just how crazy that time was. I was fresh off a divorce, dating someone new, and living like a semi-functional alcoholic Peter Pan. A group of about five friends simply refer to 1999-2000 as "The Decadence." I'm glad to put that behind me. I'm getting too old for that shit.

I sketched some drawings of a yurt. I had no idea where or how I'd build it. I'd never even seen one, but those drawings were my carrot on the end of the stick. Just get that trip under my belt, then move on to the next thing. Not that the AT was a full-on misery tour, but having another goal got me through some crappy days.

I finally built the yurt when I moved to Ohio University in Athens, Ohio, for grad school. Jess and I met at OU and lived in that yurt for two years. Down a dirt road, totally off-grid. We had oil lamps, "walking water" (as in hauling gallon jugs of drinking water from town), and a homemade wood stove. We took baths down by the creek out of 5-gallon buckets. It could be a total pain in the ass, but it was simple and quiet.

Sometimes, I really miss it.

OVERTHINKING

I'd give anything to turn my brain off.

I feel like there's a hamster in my head. Some twitchy little bastard running nonstop on a wheel. Round and round and round he goes. He's got a calculator in one paw and my calendar in the other, muttering about my bank account, gear lists, deadlines...

Screw you, stupid hamster.

I mean, it's simple, right? See that river? Paddle downstream until it turns into saltwater. Boom. Done.

Sure, there are steps. Eat, sleep, pack, and paddle, but when it comes down to it, the formula's easy: Get your ass in the canoe. Paddle. Repeat.

Before we started this trip, I did my usual thing: obsessive research. Read every book on paddling the Mississippi. Scoured every website. Read every gear review. Pored over maps, spreadsheets, and food plans. I spent *hours, days, weeks* geeking out. I told myself I was "preparing," but I wasn't.

Come on, man. That's not prep. That's just stalling.

It's busywork pretending to be preparedness. Obsessing over the perfect dry bag or comparing camp stove reviews for the fiftieth time isn't the work. It's noise. It's the same shit I did before the Appalachian Trail. It's what I often do in life. Spin wheels. Dig ruts. Burn mental gas, but never leave the driveway.

Earl Shaffer, the first guy to thru-hike the Appalachian Trail, said he "wanted to walk the war out of his system." He'd hiked sections before the war with his buddy Walt. Walt never came back from the war.

Grandma Gatewood, the first woman to thru-hike the Appalachian Trail, hiked the trail in tennis shoes and carried her gear in a sack over her shoulder. She was 67.

Just. Keep. Paddling.

It really is that damn simple.

THE HEAVY INSIDE

"I guess it comes down to a simple choice, really. Get busy living, or get busy dying."

    Andy Dufresne, Shawshank Redemption

Been thinking about Dad a lot today. My first memory is watching him hit the floor with a dull thud after the heart attack, then chasing after my sister when she ran to find Mom. Heavy stuff. He was thirty-nine. I was three.

I wonder what he'd think of all this if he were still around? I wonder if I'd even be doing these trips at all, for that matter.

What the hell am I doing out here? Shouldn't I do the respectable thing and get a real job instead of paddling all summer? Wouldn't it be easier to settle down and head down the road everyone else is traveling?

I feel like I've got a foot on two trains heading in opposite directions, and I can't straddle them forever. If I stick with the PhD, maybe I'll land a decent university job with a little time to sneak outside. Then again, plenty of professors chasing tenure seem burnt out and bitter.

The other path has me working random jobs and piecing together the things that make me tick. An old friend once said I'd either end up a graying professor or chairmaker. Honestly, I wouldn't argue with that.

I know Dad's death colors how I see all this. I could get run over by a bus tomorrow. I've already spent years doing dumb, reckless things, and I feel lucky just to still be here. I drifted for twenty years to get to this point. So...now what?

I spent my twenties floundering around from school to school, job to job, and relationship to relationship. A decade lost to decadence and depression. I've always regretted that, but I can't do anything about it now. Live and learn.

Now I'm thirty-five, winding my way down the Mississippi River with someone I'm crazy about. Not sure how I got here, but I couldn't be happier. She's smart, funny, and loves the outdoors. Quiet and reflective, loud and hilarious, and a total badass smoke show. Jess is a godsend, and I'm one lucky, lucky dude to be with her.

I can't obsess about this much more, and I'm not sure this trip is helping anything. Every day is 100% living in the moment. Not one second goes by that we're not experiencing the world around us. We're completely immersed.

That's a hard act to follow, and certainly harder to recreate in the working world. I still think about the AT every day, and I'm sure this trip will be the same.

So Dad, what do you think?

I swear this traveling stuff is a drug, but better.

It's not escaping.

It's being.

PUT ME IN COACH
DE SOTO, WISCONSIN - MILE 697

We stopped in De Soto to pick up a couple of gallons of water and some snacks. A baseball game was going on, so we decided to chill and catch the last few innings between the twelve-year-old teams from De Soto and North Crawford. Tons of folks were there. It was *the* place to be.

There was plenty of action, most of it not on the field. Toddlers played under the stands while grandfathers talked about the weather. Teenagers flirted and ignored their parents, who were sitting twenty feet away.

Kids streamed back and forth from the Kwik Trip Mart with begged money in hand and came back with sodas and candy. Kwik Trip is a team sponsor, so it balances out.

A pack of kids hunted a little green snake in the bushes. The snake didn't have a chance and ended up dangling from the end of a stick. Part Norman Rockwell. Part Lord of the Flies. We watched all this go down while we ate cold hot dogs and ice cream sandwiches. Life was good—unless you were the snake. He had a bad day.

Two teams of lanky boys gave it their all, but De Soto lost 13–1.

The crowd slowly went their separate ways. I'm guessing a few kids missed their bedtimes. I know we did.

June 13, 2005

Bottom of the 8th Inning

ANSWERS TO QUESTIONS WE'VE BEEN ASKED SO FAR

1. The Mississippi is about 2,350 miles long.
2. We paddle about 30 miles a day.
3. There are 29 locks. Yes, they're scary sometimes.
4. We camp on shore most nights.
5. We eat about 5,000 calories every day.
6. We've lost about 10 pounds between the two of us.
7. It will take about 75 days.
8. We're buying most of our food along the way.
9. The canoe is 18'6" long.
10. We haven't strangled each other, yet.

DUBUQUE, IOWA
MILE 770

Fact: I'm now officially Dubuque's biggest fan. We loved the early stretch of the river and are sad to see it go, but we're officially into the middle leg now, and Dubuque ruled hard.

We pulled in yesterday and tied up at the National Mississippi River Museum & Aquarium. Their Public Relations Director, Trish McDonald, was kind enough to put us up for the night. She's hosted a few other paddlers, one of whom stayed for a week. After spending a day here, it's easy to see why.

I'm sitting in her Victorian house, looking out over the river. In the past 24 hours, we gave press interviews, toured the museum, showered, did laundry, went to a swanky wine tasting with her friends, and drove her brand-new car for errands. That was super weird, as we haven't gone faster than a canoe in weeks. Soaked in the hot tub before bed, and even dodged what should've been a well-deserved hangover. If every day is like this in Dubuque, I'm staying.

Dubuque's got a *killer* art district vibe going for it. Downtown has some Art Deco facades from the 1920s. I'm sure the winter sucks, but I could see us ending up here.

Dubuque has been exceedingly good to us, but we have to go

before the weekend madness starts up. We stay as far away as we can from major towns and marinas on weekends. Things get hairy when boaters come out with one hand on the throttle and the other holding a beer.

Barges are like enormous dinosaurs, but are fine to be around if you give them space and respect. They're nothing to contend with compared to what we've seen from the weekend crowds. At least a barge isn't going to do donuts ten yards in front of us, pull water skiers through the shipping channel, or tow three screaming kids while weaving between pontoon boats.

Steamboats were common on the river in the mid-to-late 1800s. One of the highlights at that time was to go on the "Fashionable Tour." People would travel by train for two days to get from New York to St. Louis. They would then board a steamboat and be in Minneapolis within a week.

Four dollars got you a deck pass, but you had to bring your own food, sleep on the deck without bedding, and get off the boat twice a day to bring in cordwood for the boilers. Eight bucks got you the dining room, sleeping quarters, and probably a hot toddy to end the day.

I can't get over how the river's changed over these 770 miles. We started paddling in a creek, and now there's this huge river with barges, locks, super weird currents, and all that sort of stuff. Soon we'll be in St. Louis, past the locks, and into free-flowing water for the next 1,200 miles.

We've had our ups and downs, but this trip has surpassed every expectation. I can't wait to see what the weeks ahead will bring.

This trip aims to raise awareness for the Audubon Society's Upper Mississippi River Campaign. They own a small paddlewheeler named the Lilly Belle, which they use for interpretive programs and research. Our original plan was to meet the Lilly Belle on the river and give talks about our trip, but there wasn't enough funding to run the program. We finally got to see the Lilly Belle at the museum, and I'd love to see that program up and running again.

Trish, from the bottom of our hearts, thank you. You have no idea how much we needed this. You're the best.

Onward down the river.

June 17, 2005

MUSCATINE, IOWA, MILE 800

Today was our longest day so far—41 miles. The river keeps growing every day. Sometimes we have to cross it to dodge the barges, and lately that's been getting harder. It's not bad if we plan ahead and get inside the bends in the river, but it's a pain if we have to sprint across. Not a bad way to spend a day. Beats being in an office, any day.

Last night, we stayed with an older guy named Steve at his home near La Claire, Iowa. Steve's dad was a photographer back in the day, and we had the pleasure of seeing some of his original prints of steamboats and early river towns. Steve's office was packed with books and maps, and he was a treasure trove of information about the local area.

We stayed up well into the night talking about our trip and listening to his stories. Lack of sleep makes for rough paddling, but I wouldn't trade those moments for anything. Thanks, Steve.

We're pushing miles hard to meet Jess's parents in Hannibal this Friday. Considering the miles we're covering, we'll need a break by the time we get there, but it will be nice to see them. They're riding down from Ohio on their motorcycles. Hope the weather holds.

Over a month on the river, and I still can't believe we're out here. Sometimes I wake up at night and wonder—how did I end up with Jess on some random sandbar in the middle of the Mississippi? It's strange. It's perfect. The little stuff we see and talk about together makes the trip for me. We're learning more about each other and ourselves with each day on the water. I'm a lucky dude.

Getting through the last lock was weird. The water was hauling ass on the downstream side, so we had to be aware of what we were doing. We surfed on these huge swells rolling downriver from the lock. It's weird to be on the crest of a rolling wave and moving faster than usual. You can feel the river's awesome power underneath when it's like that.

We didn't plan to camp on this island, but I'm glad we did. It's about a mile past the lock and right in the middle of town. I feel like a fly on the wall—people don't notice us, but we can watch the moving cars and hear shouts from the shore.

We'll be about halfway soon. It seems like yesterday that we put the canoe into a little creek in Minnesota. That little creek has grown and will quickly be free-flowing to the gulf. Just a few more locks and dams are holding it back, and once we're past St. Louis, the river should be much larger and faster. I think we're ready, but anxious. It's hard to know what to expect, so we just have to take it a day at a time.

I could watch Jess paddle all day. It's sexy as hell. Every stroke is smooth, confident, and intentional. She's got a grace that most paddlers only dream of. Honestly, she's a way better paddler than I am. She's completely at home on the water, like it's where she belongs.

We're the luckiest kids in the world to be out here. I wish it'd last forever.

EFFICIENCY

So we're floating down the river, and I look down at all the stuff we're carrying. Dry bags filled with clothes and supplies, six gallons of water, and buckets filled with food. Between the gear and us, there are 600 pounds or more in the canoe.

I'm always struck by how efficient this thing is at getting people and goods from point A to point B. It's cool to think the canoe we're paddling isn't far from what was used thousands of years ago. We can reach cruising speed in a few paddle strokes and maintain that pace for hours if needed.

Sometimes, I wish life were more like that.

~

TOWN TIME

Town time is weird. As soon as we hit town, time moves at warp speed. A quick stop for ice cream turns into a four-hour expedition. I'm the guilty party most of the time. I can putz around all day looking around if left to my own devices.

Town time is fine in measured amounts, but it's best to leave before the magic wears off. It's better to have a great memory of a town before something happens and reality kicks in.

When I thru-hiked the Appalachian Trail, we had a saying that every day in a town equals a bad day of hiking. It's the same on the river. After gorging on food and lying around, we usually feel out of sync the next day. It just feels right to be in the canoe after being away from it for too long.

All in all, we'd rather be on the water than anywhere else.

Nauvoo, Illinois – Mile 986
Zero Star Review

The mayflies have been out in force. Hordes of these things are clinging to every bush, tree, and building. I'm sure the fish are eating well.

They aren't much of a problem because at least they don't bite. However, you've got to keep your mouth shut while paddling through a swarm. It's like riding a motorcycle, just at six miles an hour. Smile too much, and you'll get a mouthful of larvae to chew on.

Mayflies have a short lifespan but cram a lot of living into it. Once the nymphs leave the water, they molt twice, reproduce, and then die, all within a matter of hours. We should be lucky enough to fit that much living in.

We're hiding out tonight near the Joseph Smith Historic Center. We looked for a place to camp for hours this afternoon, but there were none to be found. I hate stealth camping like this, but we were out of options.

Paddling at night, especially when it's cloudy or foggy, is a good way to get killed. We can't see any other boats until they're right on us, and I'm sure they can't see us at all, so here we are.

The park next to the river has been hosting an annual Mormon pageant. Nauvoo was one of the largest towns in the country in the mid-1800s, primarily populated by Mormons arriving from the East. In 1846, the Mormons were forced out and headed west toward what is now Salt Lake City. Today, Nauvoo is a tourist destination for people visiting historic Mormon sites.

A few hours ago, one of the leaders here gave us permission to camp. Then, as they were leaving, he un-granted his permission.

Thanks, dude.

There's a town ordinance outlawing overnight use, and if the cops show up, we're on our own.

Worrying about getting tossed out isn't helping us get any rest tonight. The plan is to get up before dawn and get out of here before anyone shows up. What a way to spend the evening. *Yay?*

No.

This is probably gonna suck.

THE NEXT DAY...

Yeah. Last night sucked. We hid the canoe and took the bare minimum to camp with. I was frazzled. Jess was frazzled. Gah.

I passed out from sheer exhaustion sometime around midnight. Jess got up and hiked about a mile to Nauvoo State Park to take a shower and avoid the mess altogether.

Cars drove around all night, fueling the paranoia that we'd get busted for being here. Around 4 a.m., we said the hell with this, took down the tent, and snuck down to pack the canoe. We slid it into the water and set off just before dawn. Today was a blur. No sleep and a full day of just trying to unfrazzle ourselves.

Nauvoo. You get **zero** stars today. Maybe next time?

June 21, 2005

A DAY ON THE RIVER

Every day's a little different, but here's a basic rundown. My alarm goes off at 5:15 a.m., which I either ignore or sleep through. The sun starts coming up by the time we're out of the tent, and I'm singing whatever stupid song is in my head.

Some songs are just painful to have on an endless loop. Bobby Brown haunts me today, but Sir Mix-A-Lot was on shuffle last week. "I like big butts and I cannot lie..."

I mean, to be fair, I do.

Coldplay's "Clocks" plays in my head when things get hairy on the river. I'm not particularly into that band, and I couldn't name 10% of the lyrics, but it's always there, and it's comforting. The beats per minute match my paddle cadence, especially in sketchy situations when that steady piano part near the end kicks in.

> *"Home. Home. Where I wanted to go.*
> *Home. Home. Where I wanted to go."*

We pack the canoe in a semi-organized fashion depending on the weather. Clear skies = more organization. Rain? Just toss it in and go.

Each of us has a small dry bag that we keep close by for our personal items. The tent, food, and other gear are put at the bottom of the canoe to keep the weight as low as possible.

I'll fill the water bottles and prep the canoe while Jess packs the tent and checks the maps. Once on the water, we work out a mileage goal for the day. We have the time to pull this trip off between semesters, but not much more, so it helps to be organized.

After about an hour, Jess will fix breakfast, and we'll eat while drifting along. We rack up a few bonus miles during breakfast when we eat in the canoe. We're both half-awake this time of day anyway.

Filling water bottles for the day

At some point, we'll go through a lock. These giant contraptions allow barges and other large boats to travel farther upstream than they would otherwise. The Army Corps of Engineers is mandated to maintain a deep navigation channel from the Gulf of Mexico to Minneapolis.

Before the trip, we were a little worried about getting through the locks, but they've been a piece of cake for the most part. One time, we were locking through and a huge barge was right in front of the downstream gates. I thought it might eat us, but I guess it wasn't hungry that day.

Lunch is our biggest meal and the only time we cook. Most of the time, it's some sort of pasta and sauce. If I'm not careful, I might turn into a piece of macaroni soon. We usually eat lunch around 2:00 p.m. and take a long rest break. Then it's back on the river.

The first third of each day goes quickly, the middle third painfully slow, and the last third flies by. It doesn't matter if we're covering fifteen or forty miles. I have no idea why it works out that way.

Over the last few days, we've been taking longer afternoon breaks to escape the heat. Swimming in a muddy river is like a shower, right? I might sleep in a shower stall to help get the funk off when we get to Hannibal. Things are getting a little rank, and by rank, I mean I smell like a dog's butt.

We roll into camp around 8 pm. We've paddled almost to midnight (never again) and stopped as early as four. There's so much daylight now that pushing until dark is tempting. Not the greatest idea, because campsites aren't always where you think they'll be. Set up camp, settle down, and we're asleep in no time.

Jess brought a little pillow with her, but I use a wadded-up jacket instead. She's clearly the brains of this operation. Get about eight hours of sleep, and it's time to repeat the process.

Next week we'll be going through Hannibal and St. Louis. The Missouri River joins the Mississippi in St. Louis, and there are no more locks to control the river. We're nervous about riding on the free-flowing Mississippi, but are ready to see what it's all about.

Camping on a sandbar

TWO-TOWN DAY

Today was a two-town day, with plenty of town food and a good dose of rest. The "get down the river fast" part of me is being tempered by the "stop and smell the roses" side. Too much of one, and we'd burn out. Too much of the other, and we'd be on the river until Christmas.

We stopped for lunch and some water at New Boston, Illinois. We just needed a few things from the grocery store to get us through the next few days. A good thing, because there wasn't much shopping to do there. New Boston has seen better days. Many of the older homes are in poor repair, though you can tell they were beautiful back in their prime. There doesn't seem to be much industry around. The only things doing well are the churches and the bars, and they're not doing that great. Just two of each that I could see.

We spent $13.92 on groceries at the New Boston Food Center. Just a couple of drinks, canned pineapple, and some snacks. They're going out of business, so everything's discounted to clear the shelves. I picked up a few extra items we didn't really need. I figured they could use our pennies more than some grocery chain down the river.

Imagine what this place was like during its heyday. There are old grain elevators, loading ramps, huge houses, and old storefronts. What's left is on its last legs, but I bet this place was hopping not too long ago.

I walked by the Levi Willits House, built in 1856. The place had great architectural lines, and some original curved windows remained intact. It's on top of the hill with a great view of the river. Strange how it outlived the boomtown era. At some point, it was converted to apartments, and I hope the current residents can appreciate the view at least.

~

BURLINGTON, IOWA - MILE 942

We stopped in Burlington to eat lunch and pick up some sunscreen and snacks. Highs have been in the 90s every day with plenty of sun. Nothing like what we expect down in Louisiana, but hot enough all the same.

Some guy didn't believe we'd been living out of a canoe for a month because we weren't tan enough. I told the dude all we wore was rain gear for the first month, but I don't think he believed me.

Jess and I have been taking a couple of hours off every afternoon to escape the heat. The other day, we found a great beach on a sandbar, so we pulled over and went for a swim. We met some folks who worked for the local railroad while we were there. They handed us a couple of beers, and we all went floating.

We floated down with the current until the beach petered out, then hiked back to the boats and started again. They were awesome, and it was a fun way to burn a few hours. Super relaxing, and a good reminder to dial it back a notch every once in a while.

I did some math just for kicks. We each paddle about 550 strokes per mile. At 38 miles a day, that's 20,900 strokes per person, per day.

Multiply that by 2,300-something miles, and it comes out to around 1.29 million paddle strokes for each of us.

Looking at those kinds of numbers makes me want to take a nap.

June 22, 2005

1000 MILES DOWN
CANTON, MISSOURI - LOCK 21

"*So, Miss Robinson. How does it feel to have just paddled 1,000 miles?*"

"*I feel like I want some ice cream.*"

I love this woman so. Ice cream it is.

We've finally reached the 1,000-mile mark and are celebrating with some ice cream in Canton, Missouri, this afternoon. We were looking at a two-hour wait for barges to lock through, so we decided to walk into town and check out the sights. Everybody is lying low until the heat settles down, except for one guy tearing down the main drag of town on a riding lawnmower. You go, Lawnmower Man.

This trip is starting to be fueled by the need for cheap ice cream cones. Not including breaks, locks, or runs to the local gas station for ice cream, we spend about ten hours a day in the canoe. It's easy to paddle an extra ten miles if you know a tasty orange push-up is waiting for you. Those things are the best.

All this paddling is starting to wear on me. My left shoulder feels like someone is jamming a hot knife through it, and my right thumb went numb about a week ago. Jess is feeling more ragged around the edges as well. We're eating well and getting some decent sleep, but we are just getting worn down. We've got this though.

We're conducting a physiology study that measures weight loss, body fat, flexibility, strength, and blood work results as part of our research on the trip. Dr. Amanda Allen, our grad school buddy (Go Ohio Bobcats!), has helped put this study together. It hasn't been that long since we were crashing at her place, drinking cheap beer, and watching *High Fidelity* for the 29th time in her living room. The times they are a changin'.

I'm sure we've lost a few pounds, but we won't know how much until we weigh in again. I lost about twelve pounds when I hiked the Appalachian Trail, but I have no idea how that compares to paddling. I do know our bodies are changing in different ways. There's a joke among hikers about getting the "T-Rex" syndrome. You get huge legs but scrawny arms that have atrophied from a lack of use. We're seeing the opposite results. Big arms and shoulders, but our legs are wasting away. I could tear a telephone book in half, but there's no way I'd want to hike up a mountain right now. Maybe I need to make the best of it and just start walking on my hands.

Somebody asked us about conquering the river before we left. I'm not a big believer in "conquering" the outdoors myself. Mother Nature either doesn't care what you're doing out there or could squash you like a bug if she felt like it. Doing these kinds of trips has as much to do with keeping a bunch of spinning plates balanced in the air as anything else. You're juggling time, money, weather, motivation, safety, obstinance, and quite frankly, a fair amount of luck to make it to the end. The only things to be conquered on this trip will be some anxiety about the unknown and a scorching caffeine addiction. Anything else is icing on the cake.

But man, that 1,000 Mile Ice Cream was the best.

June 23, 2005

CHASING MARK TWAIN
HANNIBAL, MISSOURI - MILE 1045

We're taking a break at Bayview Campers Park in Hannibal. Jess's folks rode their motorcycles down from Ohio for a visit. We'll be back on the river tomorrow morning and head toward St. Louis and beyond.

The Bayview's owners, Roy & Sherry Wood, were gracious enough to haul our canoe back to their campground. That was a big help, as it's hard to strap a canoe on the back of a motorcycle.

Roy also arranged for two TV stations and the local radio affiliate to be at the marina. It's great to get the word out about the Audubon Society, our trip, and the folks who helped make this happen.

It was a big night of beers, banter, and bingo. They didn't know that Jess was a bingo ringer, and she walked away with a cool $17.

Jess with her winnings

We've got about seven more locks to go before we reach the free-flowing river beyond St. Louis. Our mileage should increase, as should some more things that can make the Mississippi "interesting" to small craft. I doubt we'll be bored, as we'll be dodging bigger barges, whirlpools, and stronger currents.

Last week, we paddled around forty miles a day, even with the locks, and we're hoping to average fifty miles a day once we're past St. Louis. We'll see how that pans out, but that seems like a ton of miles to cover each day.

This week marked the beginning of the dog days of summer. Highs in the upper nineties, and it'll remain that way for a while. Four weeks of cold rain, two days of spring, and now it's straight-up summer. We'll be getting up earlier to try to beat the heat and may have to take a few hours off in the afternoons to cool off.

We have to be careful not to get fried to a crisp and/or dehydrated. A severe sunburn could put the brakes on the trip, so we're going through sunscreen by the gallon. Nothing quenches soul-robbing thirst like a bottle of blood-temperature water, either.

THE END OF THE SWEET TEA DROUGHT

I grew up in the one-stoplight metropolis of Climax, NC. Sweet tea and BBQ a way of life in the South. I won't argue western vs. eastern-style barbecue, as it's best not to take contentious *religious* issues like that lightly.

If you're wondering, the correct answer is Eastern NC style, whole hog. And beef ain't BBQ.

Anyway, I hadn't seen, heard of, or sipped a drop of sweet tea in the forty-seven days since we left North Carolina for the backwoods of Minnesota. That black cloud of despair lifted yesterday.

We rode into Hannibal to take in the sights and ended up at Bubba's Catfish House for dinner. Looking over the menu of entrees, soft drinks, coffee, and beers, I found the Holy Grail—one simple, glorious sign.

TEA: SWEETENED OR UNSWEETENED

The clouds parted, and I heard a choir of angels sing the *Hallelujah Chorus* in the distance. We ordered a round of that precious nectar and then asked the waitress just to leave the whole damn pitcher. After almost a month and a half without that delicious liquid, my thirst was finally quenched.

Hallelujah indeed.

June 25, 2005

~

CLARKSVILLE, MISSOURI - MILE 1082

Sitting on a park bench near the lock while Jess is wandering around. The lock is right next to the town, and construction workers are repairing something on the dam. The time, effort, and money it takes to keep this river doing what we want is astronomical. The river today is a far cry from what it was during Mark Twain's time. Annual flooding caused massive damage back then, and the river's constantly changing dynamics made travel much more difficult.

Harold Fisk was a cartographer and geologist for the US Army Corps of Engineers back in the 1940s. In 1944, he drew an incredible set of maps illustrating the Mississippi River's "Meander Belt" at different points in time, going back centuries. The colors on the maps overlap and swirl all around, showing just how dynamic the river's march to the Gulf is. Not a bad way to spice up a government report named the *"Geological Investigation of the Alluvial Valley of the Lower Mississippi."*

Clarksville is located on the Great River Road and has several art galleries and antique shops. The Village Market is a small joint that combines a gas station, deli, and market. We had a short shopping list and walked out with just a block of cheese and some candy. No big deal. We have enough food to last a week anyway. It pays to have a generous tolerance for eating the same food all the time when your options are limited though.

June 27, 2005

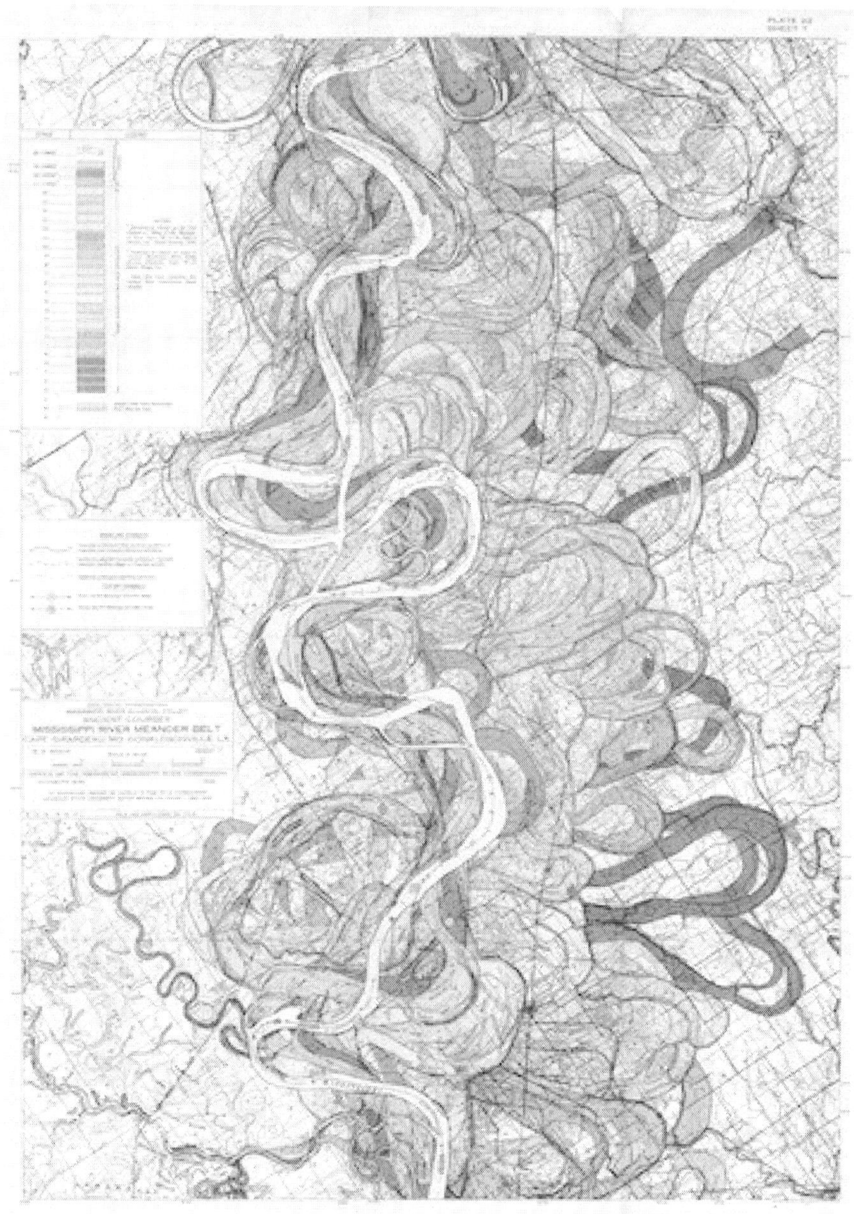

Harold Fisk Meander Map of the Mississippi River, 1944

THREE GUYS ON A RAFT

For the past week, we'd heard rumors about a floating shack making its way down the river. These guys were great. Living the dream, as it were.

We got on the water early to beat the wind while crossing the slack water pool behind the lock. Getting caught on the water during high winds isn't much fun.

We locked through and were happy to return to moving water again. We rounded a bend and saw something tied to a tree on the left bank.

"That's got to be those guys."

"You think?"

"No doubt."

We pulled up closer and saw a dude wandering around half-asleep on deck. They had a grill strapped on the roof of their shack, a couple of coolers scattered around, and the raft was custom-painted with the finest, cheapest spray paint.

They grew up on the outskirts of Minneapolis and decided to chase their dream. To build a raft and float it all the way down the Mississippi to New Orleans. They were in their mid-twenties, going through the same kind of drift I'd been in at that age. I'd half-assed my way through a few years of college without finishing, bouncing between dead-end jobs and hopping from one beer can and bed to the next. A serial monogamist, living on cereal.

I'm sure some folks called them nuts for trying to float a homemade raft down the river for no real reason. I say more power to them. In the end, it doesn't matter how far they make it. They'll have some great stories to tell later and will know what it's like to try something big. Something ridiculous. Something audacious.

In retrospect, it would have been better to drop everything I was (or wasn't) doing when I was younger and go for an adventure like these guys.

The raft looked rough around the edges, but it was holding up fine. Function over form, always. It was ten feet wide and about sixteen feet long. One of the guys, an engineering student, calculated the 55-gallon drums' flotation with the estimated raft weight and gave it the thumbs up. They lost a barrel due to the heavy waves on one of the earlier lakes and had to make repairs to ensure the others didn't suffer the same fate. One day off the water, some metal reinforcing straps, and a case of beer later, they declared it ready for travel again.

They had an 8-by-8-foot shack on top to sleep in and hide from bad weather. Three guys in a shack. Sounds cozy. And *smelly.*

Everyone seemed fine, except for one dude with a severe sunburn on his foot. It was blistered all to hell and looked brutal. I'm sure it wasn't fun to try to deal with.

"Do you guys ever get bored?" they asked. They'd been drifting and covering about 12 miles a day, and hitting most of the casinos on the way down. We'd been averaging around forty miles a day for the last week or so. I'd lose my mind just drifting on the current, but these guys were having a blast.

Godspeed and fair winds, fellas, wherever you are. I tip my beer to you.

Three Guys on a Raft

CRITTERS

Plenty of critters have hitched a free ride on this trip. All sorts of things fly, jump, crawl, or slither from under the canoe when I turn it over every morning. I let them do their thing for a few minutes and decide if they wanted to come out peacefully or if I had to chase them out. Granddaddy long-legs usually hang around the longest. Frogs bail the second we move. And then there was this little guy.

This little guy earned his seat. He launched himself in the canoe from about four feet away. I'd already had breakfast, so back into the water he went. Didn't look like much of a meal anyway.

One morning, a spider popped

out of nowhere and made its way to the bow. He liked his perch, so we just let him be. We pulled ashore for a break a few hours later, and he hopped off as if nothing had happened.

"Thanks for the ride, suckers!"

Spider riding on the canoe bow

ST. LOUIS, MISSOURI

MILE 1,157

It was going to be an extra big day. We were going past the confluence of the Missouri River, navigating through the Chain of Rocks rapids, seeing the Gateway Arch, and running the gauntlet of loading docks south of St. Louis. We also had to find a place to refill our water. The highs had been in the upper 90s all week, so running out of water was always on our minds.

LOCK 26 & THE LAST PORTAGE

Last night, we camped as close to the city as we could to get a head start on things. Yesterday, we portaged around Lock 26, the last lock on the river just north of town. We made it to the lock with an hour of daylight left and saw a line of barges waiting to pass through. I didn't want to portage anymore on this trip, but whatever. It was about two hundred yards to get over the dam and back into the river.

Portaging builds character. So, so, so much character.

We paddled to the right side of the dam to scout out things out. As we eased out of the current, the water turned an eerie shade of light green—pretty, but eerie all the same. I thought about the millions of gallons of wastewater being pumped into the river upstream. You can talk about contaminated parts per million all you want, but this was still pretty funky stuff to glide through.

The dams above Minneapolis have established portage routes, but today we'd have to wing it. Sometimes you can find a shorter route on the side opposite the lock. We paddled over, tied up the canoe, and went for a look. No luck. Nothing but a swamp full of cattails, so no shortcuts for us today.

We had to get moving if we wanted to find a place to camp before dark. We planned to camp on a nearby island, but you can't tell about those things until you get there. Sometimes an island is a sandy paradise with a pleasant grove of trees where you can camp. Other times, it's a patch of mosquito-infested mud a few inches above the water.

We decided the best portage route would be over the rocks, across a parking lot, and down the boat ramp on the other side. Portaging isn't rocket science, just necessary grunt work. Tiring, boring, and unavoidable.

Getting the gear onto shore was a challenge. The shore was steep and rocky, so I had to stand in the canoe and throw the gear to Jess. Heavier items, like the five-gallon water container, had to be carried across slick, mossy rocks. Jess would catch the gear, scramble up the bank, unload it, and then come back for the next load. We keep our life jackets on when we're running around on the riprap in case we fall. We had a paddling teacher who swore more people got hurt falling on rocks than paddling whitewater. We weren't in the mood for cracked ribs, so we heeded Mr. D's advice. Thanks, Ron.

Once all the big gear was out, we still had to deal with the little stuff. We corralled all the half-used tubes of sunscreen, water bottles, sandals, and other junk into a big mesh bag. I don't know where half this stuff comes from, but I think it breeds when we're not looking.

Slowly but surely, the pile of gear made it to the boat ramp. If we're motivated, we can get everything over in two big trips. After a long day's paddle, neither wanted to carry extra-heavy loads. Carrying less gear means more trips back and forth, but with a portage this short, that's a fair trade-off.

The path to the ramp was nasty, beer cans, broken glass, and a big pile of rotting carp oozed beside the trail. The carp were a stinky reminder to move faster every time we passed by.

Soon, we had schlepped everything over except the canoe. Early on in the trip, Jess and I would carry the canoe by the handles at each end. By the end of a long portage, you'd feel like one arm was longer than the other. Eventually, I wised up and found it easier to carry it by myself on my shoulders.

Again, portaging builds character.

Oh my god, so much character.

After packing up, we set off for an island about an hour away. We've always made it a point to camp away from civilization whenever possible. Besides the safety issues, it's too loud to get any sleep. I've stayed awake a few nights listening to traffic, trains, and other town noises when we camped too close. It's neat that nobody knows you're there, but no sleep sure makes for a long day of paddling.

Today, we were off at sunrise.

MISSOURI RIVER CONFLUENCE

So many times, what I thought a place would look like didn't jive with reality. The Missouri and Ohio rivers are the largest tributaries flowing into the Mississippi. My only thoughts were of boiling waters, unpredictable currents, and whirlpools big enough to suck the canoe under if we paddled too close.

The hair was up on the back of my neck as we approached the confluence. We both wanted to see what the water was doing before diving in. Truth be told, I had to go to the bathroom in the worst way too. Go figure.

We pulled the canoe over to the right side of the river and tied it to the rocks as best we could. A path led up to a small monument overlooking the confluence of the two rivers.

When we reached the top of the knoll, we turned around to take in the scene. Incredible. Simply incredible. Just thinking about the history of these two rivers gave me goosebumps. How many people have stood at this exact point before? Thousands? Millions? Lewis and Clark's party camped here in 1804 on their way up the Missouri. Native Americans beat them there by a few thousand years.

Mississippi - Missouri River Confluence

If you're going upstream, you have to make a simple decision. Left? Right? Left up the Missouri takes you through the Great

Plains and ends up at its source in Montana. Go right up the Mississippi, and you go through the heartland, ending up in Minnesota.

It's mind-boggling to think about this stuff. Right in front of us are the waters collected from 32 states and 2 Canadian provinces. More than a million square miles of land drain into it. That's a damn massive watershed.

We watched as the clearer waters of the Missouri mixed with the muddy waters of the Mississippi. The boils at the confluence didn't seem too wild today, but we were going to give them plenty of respect and room. We pushed the canoe into the water and headed directly to the middle of the main channel. Easy peasy, lemon squeezy. On to St. Louis, the Arch, and beyond.

CHAIN OF ROCKS

One of the things I'd read about before the trip was the infamous Chain of Rocks in St. Louis. The Chain of Rocks is a large limestone ledge that spans the entire river, creating rapids from one bank to the other. A canal bypasses it now, but it was a major impediment to river travel in large boats for hundreds of years.

The canal is a no-go for canoes and kayaks, as it's too narrow with too many barges, so over the Chain you go. Depending on the water level, it can be easy, or...not. There are tons of concrete and rebar in that stretch from bank to bank from previous construction projects, so that's fun. At higher water levels, you'll just float over all that stuff. At lower levels like we're at, everything's in play, and you damn sure better be careful. Folks drown there regularly. We didn't want to drown today.

We could hear the rapids as we approached the bridge just upstream. We pulled over to the right side and played on the bank for a bit before doing the serious work of scouting the rapids. The river was pretty low, which didn't help the situation.

We decided to portage the first 30 yards of the more squirrely mess and go from there. Schlepping all our gear over a bunch of rocks builds character. We've got character for days now.

Chain of Rocks, St. Louis MO

We planned our route through the rest of the rapids, repacked the canoe, tied everything down, and hoped for the best. As I've said before, Jess is a way better paddler than I am and I have complete faith in her, but I was scared shitless. Confident, but shitless. We've got this.

I pushed us off, hopped in, and we headed downstream. A few bumps here and there, and we were into the river proper. We followed the "tongue" of the waves as best we could, took on some water at the biggest drop, and then we were through. The water rushed by, and we were flying downriver. We lived to paddle another day.

(*Note to future paddlers: There is an actual portage route on river left - JP*)

THE GATEWAY ARCH

The St. Louis Gateway Arch is 630 feet tall and billed as The Gateway to the West. It's the big stainless steel thing next to the river. Can't miss it.

Earlier, we arranged to meet with a few camera crews to discuss our journey, the Audubon Society's mission, and all that. It was already a hundred degrees and scorching hot. We also hoped to find a place to refill our water jugs. We were a little early, so Jess went to find some burgers while I waited with the canoe.

After standing in line for an hour, Jess came back with a bag of burgers, but still no news crew. We ate our lunch, putzed around for a bit, looked for water, straightened the gear, and finally gave up on them. Still no water, but we thought we could catch the Coast Guard station downstream in the industrial dock area.

The Gateway Arch

RUNNING THE GAUNTLET: THE INDUSTRIAL DOCKS

The last part of getting through St. Louis was more than I expected. More of what?

Everything.

Because the confluence of the Missouri is just upstream, every barge going up or down either the Mississippi or the Missouri motors through St. Louis. There are about forty-eight docks to negotiate in ten miles. The barge traffic was heavy, but those are easy enough to deal with if you're paying attention. I mean, it's tough to miss a barge coming at you. All the docks and barges tied to each side of the river make a solid wall for waves to bounce off. These reflecting waves pile up on each other, get larger and faster, and can be completely unpredictable.

We were managing fine until a half dozen large cabin cruisers came flying by. These yachts throw a bigger wake than the barges most of the time, and ALWAYS, ALWAYS, ALWAYS travel in groups. I doubt they can go to the bathroom without a few wingmen telling them how awesome they are. Anyways...

Things got chaotic fast. There was already a ton of barge traffic, the river was flowing fast, and the wave action was bananas. Huge reflecting waves were bouncing everywhere, and when that bunch of yahoos flew by us, we got sideways to the current and headed into the main channel more than once. The feeling of being that out of control sucked, but we pulled it together, paddled for all we were worth, and got headed in the right direction.

After that excitement, we made our way down the river and onto our sandbar campsite. Most nights we're camped out on sandbars now. We slept like the dead and were happy we made it through okay.

Getting through St. Louis is a big psychological boost. It's about halfway down, and more importantly, there are no more locks to go through the rest of the way. From now on, the river is free-flowing to the Gulf. The current should speed up so we can make a few more miles every day. I spoke to a few folks who have paddled the river, and they all mentioned paddling fifty-mile days below St. Louis. I'll believe it when I see it. That seems so much faster than we've been doing, but we'll see.

Onward, in one piece.

June 29, 2005

TWENTY YEARS LATER...

Look, we're not hardasses by any stretch. Jess and I are solid paddlers. We've led trips, taught classes, and all that sort of thing. Not on the Olympic team, but not flipping the canoe at every ripple either. Looking back twenty years later, there were only a handful of moments on the Mississippi that genuinely scared me. This was one of them.

Dumping the canoe in Sauk Rapids would've been beyond annoying, but it wouldn't have put us in real danger. We'd get dumped out and spit downstream, but we usually tied our gear in well enough that we wouldn't lose anything. Yes, it would have been a monumental pain in the ass, but that's about it.

Going through St. Louis was different. In retrospect, Chain of Rocks was straightforward and more of a mind game than anything. Going past the Arch and into the industrial section? Now THAT was super sketchy. We were doing fine until the cabin cruisers came screaming through. Then it was a hot mess of reflecting waves, barges, walls, weird currents, and us two just trying to get downstream without being killed. Getting sucked under a barge was a real possibility, and there'd be no coming back from that.

PART THREE

THE LOWER MISSISSIPPI AND ATCHAFALAYA RIVERS

CHESTER, ILLINOIS
MILE 1,224

Yesterday we visited Herculaneum, Missouri, to refill our water containers, snag breakfast, and resupply. The locals call it "Herky." Let's be honest, we mostly went because of the name. How can you pass up a place called Herculaneum? You can't, and you shouldn't.

The beach area by the river looked like the local hangout, with beer cans and exploded fireworks scattered everywhere. We pulled to shore, hid the canoe, and hoofed it into town.

After passing an old industrial area, we found the building with the combined city hall, police, and county business offices. We asked for directions to the closest breakfast joint and were walking off when Herculaneum's mayor, John Chamis, flagged us down.

Ten minutes later, we were being shuttled to a Jack-in-the-Box and brought back for the royal treatment.

They handed over a copy of the city's history, along with t-shirts, pins, and bandanas featuring the city logo. That pin went straight onto my PFD. Super nice folks.

Not twenty-four hours after being stood up for three interviews in St. Louis, I'm sitting in the mayor's chair calling my mom. The only thing that could have topped that would have been grabbing a beer at the Bucket of Blood Saloon. Too bad that place closed in 1850. Great name for a bar, and I bet some serious shit went down there.

Seeing the confluence of North America's two largest rivers was mind-blowing. The silty waters of the Missouri combined with the brown mud of the Mississippi over the course of several hundred yards. Next up is the Ohio River, which we should hit in about three days.

There are no more locks to pass through, and now we're paddling about six miles per hour. I think we'll be able to do those fifty-mile days I'd read about without killing ourselves if the river stays like this. Pulling those kinds of miles seemed outrageous a few weeks ago when we were slogging through the wetlands. I'll believe it when I see it.

Herculaneum, MO pin on my PFD

Everything keeps getting BIGGER. The width of the river, the weirdness of the currents, and the size of the barges. Recreational boats have all but disappeared. It's just fishing boats, monster barges, and us now. It's desolate. It's wild. It's beautiful. The Big Ditch, so they say.

Over the next week, we'll greet the Ohio River and reach Memphis. We're making good time and, unbelievably, are on schedule to finish in time to return to school. I'm never on time for anything. There must be something in the water.

July 1, 2005

CAPE GIRARDEAU, MISSOURI

MILE 1,303

We lucked out and got adopted again in Cape Girardeau. When we need it most, a benevolent stranger comes out of nowhere to boost us up. I have no idea how or why this happens, but I won't fight it.

Dr. Tom Holman from Southeast Missouri State University offered us a place to stay, homemade food, and hot showers. We could use all three right now, especially the showers. The weather has been scorching, and we need the rest. Every mile takes a little more out of us, so it's time to throttle down some and toss the schedule out the window.

We arrived in Cape Girardeau a few hours early, unsure of the best place to land. Our map showed a boat ramp upstream of town, but we either didn't see it or the map was wrong. So it goes.

We paddled up a small creek and hid the canoe, then walked and talked a couple of miles into town to kill some time until Tom could pick us up. I love our walks and talks.

Cape Girardeau isn't a particularly wealthy town, and many of the houses on the outskirts were pretty beat up. However, the closer we got to downtown, the better things began to look. There were several beautiful old buildings, and the mural on the flood wall was incredibly detailed. It was very cool to see a river town embracing its history.

A cookout, plenty of chill time, a huge breakfast, and then we were ready to get back on the water. Tom, thank you. You're an angel, and your family was so kind to take us in for the evening.

The Mississippi Queen Riverboat

OHIO RIVER CONFLUENCE
MILE 1,357

We finally made it to the last major confluence—the Ohio River. It runs nearly a thousand miles to get here from Pittsburgh. For years, I would think about the Ohio River's march to the Mississippi every time we crossed the bridge at Ravenswood, West Virginia on the way to or from weekend paddling trips in grad school.

We could feel the pull of the water as we approached the confluence. Before heading into it, we wanted to scout the river. We pulled over and hiked up to Fort Defiance State Park. From the observation tower, we could see where the two rivers meet.

The park was trashed after the weekend. Beer bottles, fast food bags, and broken coolers were scattered everywhere. We did find a working spigot at the far end of the park. The brown water didn't taste great, but at least it was cold.

On the way back, we met a group of motorcyclists out for a day trip. Meeting strangers along the way is one of my favorite parts of the trip. Just sharing a bit of someone's life reminds me that people are just people. Everyone has their demons, worries, thrills, and sorrows. We're all here on this big blue marble for one spin. You'd better make the best of it.

I still can't believe we've made it this far. Paddling ten hours a day is taking its toll. My left shoulder is still aching, and I'm eating ibuprofen like candy to keep the pain down. Push through? Rest? I'm worried this shoulder might take us off the river for good.

Getting back into the river was a little tricky. We watched the barges struggle to get upstream where the rivers joined. Reading the river ahead of time gave us a chance to make a plan. We chose our line and made adjustments on the fly. The river does what it wants. All you can do is watch, plan, and react.

Once we were through the confluence, I snuck a peek behind. The two muddy rivers danced for hundreds of yards as their waters blended. The eddies, small whirlpools, and boiling water were strangely calming. In less than a month, we'll watch the Mississippi empty into the Gulf of Mexico.

This marks the end of our navigation map set. A few days ago we grabbed a gas station map, and that's going to have to do until Memphis, where we'll (hopefully) snag the rest from the Corps of Engineers. I mean, we've crisscrossed the country before with paper maps and maybe a AAA Trip Guide, but this is different. Out here there aren't any signs that say, "Restaurant and water, 2 miles ahead." Should be...interesting?

Eight hundred more miles. I'm gobsmacked.

Onward to Memphis.

TROUBLE AT NEW MADRID BEND

MILE 1,421

"Y'all gonna die!"
"There's whirlpools down there."
"You's a dead man!"

Thanks, assholes.

Today was the first day that we felt threatened by other people on the river. We've hiked and paddled thousands of miles, and nearly every interaction has been positive. It's that 0.1% that always sticks out.

So today we went around New Madrid Bend. It's a huge oxbow where the river almost connects to itself. If you look at a map, you'd think you could portage across and make a shortcut, but that's not happening. The river was full and moving fast, but nothing unusual. Barges stayed in the channel, and we stayed just to the inside while avoiding the wing dams. Everything was cool until we met two groups of rednecks in oversized jon boats.

Now, we've heard we were going to die several times down the river, mostly from folks who don't look like they've traveled much outside their own zip code. I've heard the same thing while hiking on the AT and on other trips. I have no idea what the hell these people are scared of, but they seem to be scared of everything.

We were paddling along, and these dudes came all the way across the river to cruise right by us and yell. There's no one else out here, so when you see someone bee-lining for you, it's either gonna be really good or really bad. In this case, there wasn't anything good about what was happening. Jess snuck a quick picture and got their boat numbers, then hid the camera in case we needed it later.

They came by again, beers in hand, yelling and just being general assholes. We made our way to shore—if things went sideways, we'd rather handle it on land than in the water. One last pass, and one last bunch of yells, and it was over. A little while later, we saw one boat towing another, so these geniuses must have run out of gas.

Bless their hearts.

July 5, 2005

MUSINGS 11

ASHES TO ASHES - MILE 1,493

We've been carrying some precious cargo since we left Hannibal. Jess's mom brought down her mother's ashes so we could return her to the river. It's an honor and very humbling to be trusted with this.

Last night, we decided our campsite would be the right place to release her ashes. We woke up at dawn, walked out to the river, lit a candle, and scattered her ashes in the water. It was a powerful moment I'll never forget.

Jess and I have grown even closer in the past few weeks. We spend twenty-four hours a day together and depend on each other in all kinds of ways. We've shared many experiences, but this was a truly special moment. Again, a very humbling experience. It's comforting to think that Helen will join us to the Gulf. She always enjoyed the river. Now she'll always be a part of it.

Throughout this trip, we've been overwhelmed by the compassion and love shown to us. We've always felt this was a collective journey with many people involved, and we're just the two lucky ones in the canoe. Someday I hope to repay the kindness we've received.

Every day has been a new adventure, and I wake up thankful for another chance to make the memories. I hope to remember these things before the noise of everyday life drowns them out.

TOO CLOSE FOR COMFORT?

The first thing people always ask us is "how haven't we *killed* each other yet?" One dude said he loved his wife, but he'd rather chew off his right foot than be around her for that long. Come to think about it, that's been a common sentiment from folks we've met.

Jess and I enjoy spending time together and get along well in close quarters. Living out of a tent for a few months isn't that far of a stretch from our grad school days. We met at Ohio University while getting our master's degrees. I was living in a yurt I'd built outside of town—no power, no water, oil lamps, the whole bit.

We spent two years in that 250-square-foot palace and did just fine. After that, bathing out of a five-gallon bucket is sort of old hat. Not that I don't enjoy hot water when we have it, but there are plenty of times when I miss reading by oil lamps and listening to the wind and rain.

There hasn't been much alone time during the trip, that's for sure. We're in the canoe for about ten to twelve hours every day. There's always something to do, like setting up camp, cooking, resupplying, and hauling clean water. It's no wonder some folks call canoes "divorce machines."

After finishing the chores, I usually go for a short walk with my tape recorder and talk about the day. It gives me a little space, and gives Jess a break from my smelly self.

Being in close proximity all the time is just another part of the journey. Our 5'x7' tent is our home every night. The canoe is around eighteen feet long. The deal is she gets the front half, and I get the back. Fortunately, the canoe is long enough that we can't smack each other with paddles. Fortunately for me, at least.

Back in the real world, you can slam the door and walk away to blow off steam. That doesn't work out here because there's no door to slam, and you'd get all wet and cold if you tried. Then you'd be cold, wet, *and* pissed off.

So we deal with it.

There are plenty of ways of dealing with things—some effective, some less so. You can be silent and brood, but that won't last long. If nothing else, we have to talk about how to dodge the next barge. Next, we could just pretend nothing's the matter. That only works until someone blows up over something stupid later on.

The best option is to take that moment of reflection and get to the heart of the matter. Those moments of reflection run the gamut from

"Hey sweetie, what's the matter?"

to

"What in the %$&#! is wrong with you?!"

To be sure, some of our moments of reflection could be heard five miles away.

Eventually, the junk gets aired out, and things settle down. While we've had our "moments of reflection," the result is that we're stronger as a couple. I can't imagine going on this trip with anyone else.

I'm one lucky dude.

THE KINDNESS EQUATION

One of the things that draws me to traveling is the people I meet. Strangers at first, but friends by the time you part ways.

It's a different experience when traveling by foot, bike, or small boat. You're completely exposed to the elements and more dependent on others than at any other time.

Call it trail magic, the traveler's code, or whatever. Something happens when you walk into town and see folks who smile, nod, or want to help before they even know your name.

There is always some give and take. You might meet someone while sorting through your gear, opening mail at the post office, or walking to the grocery store to restock. They ask what you're doing, and pretty soon they're full of questions about the trip. It's not uncommon to get "kidnapped" and taken to meet other folks, have a cup of coffee, or stay overnight at someone's house.

It's humbling when someone gives you the keys to their house and tells you to lock up when you leave. These folks don't know you from Adam, but they trust you with everything.

I've always felt a little guilty about it. What did I do to deserve this kindness? What can I offer in return? The best way I can make this equation work in my head is to hope we've given them something to talk about for a while. Something unexpected that landed in their laps while they were going out to pick up a gallon of milk.

These unplanned meetings are some of the best experiences for me. Like getting the grand tour of Herculaneum after we stopped to fill our water jugs. Or being taken in for the night by folks as we paddle past their house. Or hopping into a fancy car and being driven to a stranger's place for showers. It's a trip.

The love and concern we receive is incredible, and it gives me faith in the world. I just hope these folks know how much we appreciate their kindness. Again, it's a humbling experience.

I guess the best way to repay it is to pass it on. To be that stranger for someone else, out of the blue. I hope to get the chance sometime soon.

STORMY MONDAY

We sometimes check the weather radio while getting ready in the morning. Most of the time, it's the same old thing: hot, maybe thunderstorms, blah blah blah. There's nothing you can do about it, so we just keep plugging away.

But today, we were really glad we turned that thing on.

It alerted us that a massive string of storms was blowing through our area. Big wind, heavy rain, and tons of lightning. We kept an eye on the sky as the gray clouds to the west got darker and darker. Not going to lie. I love spooky weather like that. I'm in my happy place when the weather forecast says "Cloudy, with a good chance of dying." Yes, I'm probably going to get hit by lightning while doing something stupid one day.

We started looking for a place to hide, but there weren't many options. Finally, we came across an abandoned barge that was half-destroyed but would make a good shelter if needed. We pulled the canoe over to see if we could get into the woods behind it.

The woods were choked with weeds and briars, but we finally found a flat spot just big enough to squeeze in the tent. This would have to do. Jess pitched the tent while I wrestled the canoe into the woods and tied it to a couple of trees. We dove into the tent, zipped it up, and waited.

We could hear the wind building in the distance, and then it hit like a train. Crazy wind, blinding rain, and nonstop lightning. Branches flew everywhere and crashed all around us. Sketchy, sketchy, sketchy.

Jess said, "If I have to get crushed inside a tent, I'm glad it's with you."

Morbid. Sweet. Funny. I do love her so.

The last time we were in something like this was in our yurt. A monster lightning storm burst all around us one night. The air cracked, and you could smell the ozone. One bolt hit so close I thought it had nailed the car.

We got really lucky today. Branches landed a couple of feet from the tent, and trees were down all over the place. The birds were pissed. We went to check on the canoe. Still there. That was nice.

We met a couple of guys who weren't so lucky. They were taking a sailboat down the river, recording a video, and hoping to pitch it as a movie. They still had their sails up when the squall hit, and it broke their mast. Last we heard, they were heading to Memphis to pick up the boat trailer, and their trip was over. It's a shame. We liked those dudes.

Today, we dodged a bullet. It wouldn't have been good times if we'd been on the water when that front hit. Our senses get better the more time we spend outside. You're more in tune with your surroundings. The weather, smells, winds, birds, and crickets. All of it.

Another storm down. More to come?

Onward.

THE HUMAN SCALE OF TRAVEL
BOREDOM, RITUALS, AND ESCAPE

Traveling by foot or canoe shrinks the world down. Standing next to a train watching it go by, I can't help but be impressed by its size—railcars carrying tons of gravel or whatever rolling down the track, screaming against the rails. The ground shakes as they pass by. Yet when I'm not out in the field, I don't notice these behemoths. I just tune them out completely.

Back home, there's a train track about 1/2 mile from our apartment. Now and then, I hear a whistle, but that's about the extent of it. I like the feeling of getting knocked back down in scale. Egos, jobs, home life, and responsibilities? All those things just insulate us from the world.

In the grand scheme of things, we're just a small bit of flesh, on a small planet, spinning in a small galaxy out into this vast sea of eternity. And you know what? That's fine with me.

~

BOREDOM

Boredom's one of the hardest parts of long trips, and nobody ever talks about it. People imagine constant inspiration from nature's beauty, but I've spent plenty of hours just staring at clouds or watching a blob of gelatinous larvae roll around in goo.

Most of the time there's enough happening to keep your mind busy. Other times, not so much. That's when you start inventing mental and physical diversions until the next shiny thing comes along. I've had one-sided conversations with chipmunks, rocks, mud, trees, and that same blob of larvae. They nodded a lot, but I think it was just the wriggling.

So we make up games.

Jess and I play games of "throw the rock" and "jump over the creek" to pass the time. Some folks write in their journal. Some folks sing. I've probably skipped two hundred pounds of rocks. Anything to keep my brain from melting and leaking out of my ears. I might need that thing later.

Today, we set up camp a little earlier than usual and just messed around. Skipped some rocks. Took some pictures. Walked. Talked. Chilled.

Today was a jump the creek day.

And it was awesome.

Jump the Creek Day

BARGES

Before we started, I had never seen a river barge up close, much less paddled next to one. It's hard to describe just how big these things are, but here goes. A river barge, or "tow barge," consists of the barge itself plus the boat that pushes or pulls it. The barge is what carries coal, gravel, soybeans, corn, or whatever else needs to be moved, and a typical setup is a 3x5 formation: three barges wide and five long. This whole mass is pushed by the towboat.

Why call it a towboat if it's pushing? Way back when, barges were often towed from shore by oxen or horses, and later by powered boats. As the boats got bigger, they moved to the back where they had more control. Towboats eventually became pushboats, but the name stuck. Clear as mud?

Barges on the river are enormous, but they don't usually cause many problems if you keep an eye out for them. They're not going to spin a 360 in front of you, but they do throw big wakes from the sides and rear. You have to hit those waves at the right angle or risk flipping your canoe.

We picked up a pamphlet from one of the locks upstream that showed just how efficiently barges move goods. One barge alone can hold 1,500 tons of cargo, or approximately 453,600 gallons of fuel. A typical tractor-trailer truck typically carries 26 tons, while a railroad jumper car can hold about 112 tons.

A standard 3x5 tow, with 15 barges lashed together, carries as much as 200 train cars or 870 semi-trucks. That's a whole bunch of beans!

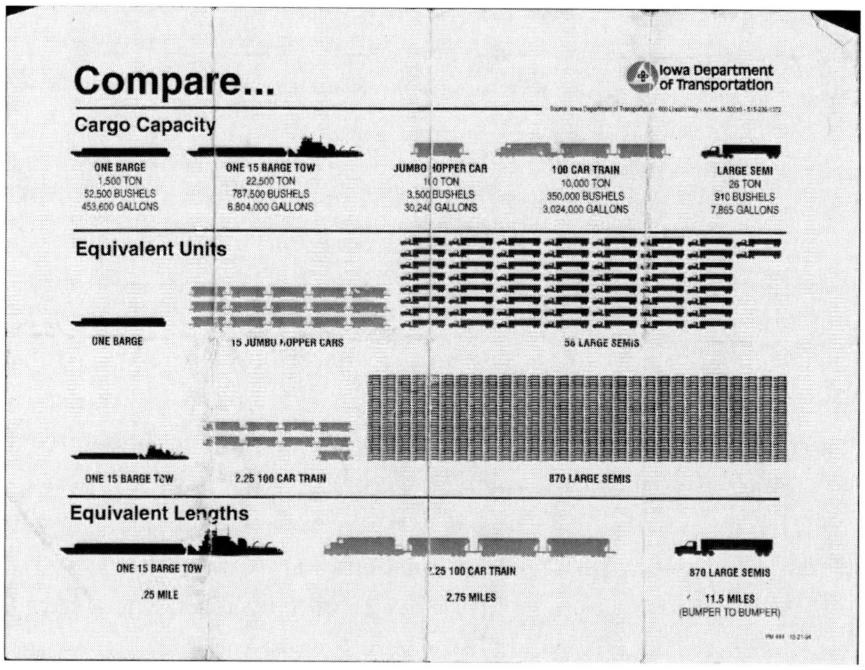

Barge Comparison Chart

TEN USES FOR A BAILER

We have nothing to do but talk as we paddle down the river all day. Talk about this. Talk about that. Sometimes it'd be nice to have a radio, but at least someone else is around to talk with. Hours are spent figuring out the world's problems or other things that don't get much attention back home. Most of the time, our talks aren't quite so deep.

We have a couple of bailers onboard to empty the water that gets into the canoe. Nothing fancy, just the tops cut off of one-gallon milk jugs. Simple, cheap, and effective. My kind of gear.

After paddling fourteen hundred-something miles, I'm convinced a bailer can be used for just about anything. Someone once said that with a bailer and some duct tape, you could move the world. Something like that, at least.

Anyway, here are a few things we came up with.

1. Urinal
2. Megaphone (cap off)
3. Rain gauge
4. Scoop
5. Quiet drum
6. Funnel
7. Cup
8. Bowl
9. Hat
10. And, of course, a plain old bailer

~

RITUALS AND LUXURIES

Little things make a world of difference when you're laying your head down in a new place each night. We take an inflatable pink flamingo along on every trip. Flo, the Guard Flamingo, watches over us in every storm. We haven't died yet, so I guess she's doing her job. She's the best flamingo.

My buddy Matt gave me a corncob pipe. I smoke it maybe a dozen times a year, but that pipe usually makes the cut when I'm packing for a trip. It keeps the bugs down, and I like writing in my journal with it handy. It gives the writing an authentic, aromatic flavor when I dribble pipe juice on the page.

I try to finish each day with a Peppermint Patty. They bring back memories of sitting on a cold, wet log in the woods, gently peeling back the wrapper and savoring the pepperminty scent. I slowly eat away those delicious chocolate edges, then wolf down the rest. No matter how crappy the day might be, everything's alright as long as there is a patty waiting for me. Those things have some serious mojo.

Setting up the tent the same way each night is another part of our routine. My watch and headlamp are always wrapped around a water bottle. That bottle gets put next to my sandals. Jess puts her book and glasses in the gear loft, and her headlamp stays in the mesh pocket by her head. I sleep on the left side of the tent. She sleeps on the right.

It's our home.

~

YOU GOTTA RUN TO SOMETHING

I've been thinking about this whole 'running to something versus running from something' thing today. There's a lot of research on why people take long-distance trips. I even wrote my master's thesis on it. One constant is that most people taking these sorts of trips are in a transitional phase of their lives. It could be a divorce, graduation, job loss, or whatever. Dig a little deeper, and you get to the real motivation. Why do they *stay* out there? That's where the good stuff is.

When I hiked the Appalachian Trail, I was 30 years old, fresh off a divorce. Working a dead-end job and going nowhere. I'd thought about hiking the AT for 10 years, and there wasn't a better time to do it. What did I have to lose? Life, relationships, job prospects? All of that was shit. I felt like a loser, and I wanted to prove to myself that I could finally finish something.

That trip, I was running *from* something. Lots of things.

This trip's different. I'm running to something. And it feels good. After I crawled off Springer Mountain and finished the AT, I made a promise to do something big every five years. Build a house, get married, fly to the moon—whatever. Just a reminder not to slide into ruts and spend my whole life spinning my wheels.

Jess and I are doing media work this trip with the Audubon Society, and I'm also writing a series of newspaper articles. We love introducing folks to the river, the idea of a big trip, and Audubon's programs, especially what they're doing on the Upper Mississippi. I'm glad we're doing this. It feels exactly like what I need to be doing right now.

You never get away from what you're running from. Until you face your demons, you're not going anywhere.

Now running *to* something? *That's* the good stuff.

WIDE AWAKE

I choose to listen to the river for a while, thinking river thoughts, before joining the night and the stars.
  -Ed Abbey

2 a.m. I'm wide awake.

Just went for a walk on the sandbar and sat by the river to relax. It's so quiet out here right now. Nothing but a few critters rustling around in the woods behind us and waves lapping the shoreline. I'd like to bottle this moment for later.

It's a crystal clear night, and the stars are super bright. Reminds me of being a kid, walking out into the hay field and just staring at the stars forever. I can still smell the fresh-cut alfalfa and see the lightning bugs everywhere. I was maybe thirteen, stuck in my head like always, just needing a little peace.

A barge went by a little while ago, scanning the river with its incredibly bright spotlight. They're looking for their routes between the buoys for safe passage up the river. Sometimes they'll scan the river and pause for a few moments on our campsite. Maybe it's the reflective tape on our canoe. Or maybe they're just bored and messing with us. Knowing we're not the only folks out here is reassuring.

The desolation this past week has been heavy. It's just us and the barges. You can hear the waves lapping on the shore at night, and every once in a while, a fish will jump. It's nice and calm right now, and I love it.

I've got to try to get some rest. Paddling on two hours of sleep is pure misery. Lots more miles to go.

TAR PITS AND A SAND BAR SANCUARY

MILE 1,566

DINOSAUR IN A TAR PIT

We decided to take a break and pulled over to the left side of the river. The water moved slowly, and we bumped the canoe into the mud about 30 feet from shore. We were stuck in a mud flat—nothing but thick, gray, super-sticky mud under the canoe. I decided to take a chance and hopped into the mud/water/goo combo. Jess stayed in the canoe and laughed.

Because she's smart.

And I'm...me.

I immediately got stuck. Like, stuck-stuck. Luckily, I didn't have my sandals on, because those things would've surely been sucked down and lost. We go days without wearing sandals now, usually leaving them in the canoe unless we are heading into town. Kinda nice, really.

Slowly, but ponderously, I worked my right leg free. Then the left. Then the right again. I was laughing, but felt like a lumbering

151

dinosaur wandering into the La Brea tar pits. Jess, of course, captured my stupidity on film for posterity.

No victory dance. I was just happy to be on solidish ground. No way Jess was getting out of the canoe, because that would've been stupid. Then I did it all again, only in reverse.

One step.

Two step.

Three step.

Goo step.

This debacle reminded me of a movie I watched as a kid. We'd watch movies every afternoon after church let out. Kelly, my step-dad, was a big Western fan. Still is. Anyway, *Sometimes a Great Notion* came on. There's a scene where a guy gets trapped under a massive log in a rising river. His brother tries to move it, but it won't budge.

As the river rises, the trapped guy goes under. His brother gave him mouth-to-mouth for a while, but eventually the guy drowned.

No idea why that might've been on my mind.

Slogged back to the canoe and washed off the worst of the stinking muck with the bailer.

Funny at the time, but kinda creepy.

Out here, actions can have *real* consequences.

Onward to Memphis and beyond.

BURIED ALIVE ON A SANDBAR

Another afternoon, another crazy-ass storm. Thankfully, we kept an eye on the weather and saw this one coming. As the sky grew darker, we hauled butt to a sandbar.

We pulled the canoe up and walked around. Our options were slim, so we dug a couple of shallow body-size holes in the sand, set down our sleeping pads, and flopped under the tarp like a pair of sweaty baked potatoes.

Yeah, it was hot.

It hit us with screaming wind, a wall of rain, and then, dead calm. The whole time, we were laughing at how fun and ridiculous it was.

It was the best.

RIDING THE STORM OUT
OXFORD, MISSISSIPPI

As the crow flies, Oxford is about 70 miles from the Mississippi River. So why the hell are we here?

We got off the river a few days ago to dodge Hurricane Dennis. After we tied up the canoe at the Memphis Yacht Club (thank you, thank you!), we headed to Beale Street for BBQ and sightseeing, then struck out, again, trying to get maps at the Corps of Engineers office. Finally, we went to a delightfully air-conditioned movie theater to catch Brad Pitt and Angelina Jolie's magnum opus, *Mr. and Mrs. Smith.*

Dr. Matt Zuefle, my college advisor and our dear friend, came up from Oxford and scooped us up. We've known Matt and his fiancée, Laura, for years, and it's been great to hang out with them. He's teaching at the University of Mississippi now, and she's doing development work there. They're both wickedly smart and funny as hell. We love both of them to pieces. I consider Matt my older brother in many ways.

I'm getting antsy from just sitting around. We're used to being in the canoe all day, and all this lounging feels weird. Granted, we haven't taken a real day off in ages and need the rest, but this isn't exactly what I had in mind.

So here's the routine for the last couple of days.

- 3:00 a.m. Wake up confused about where I am. Stumble to the bathroom just in time.
- 7:00 a.m. Roll off the air mattress. Stare around aimlessly and try to remember where I am again.
- 7:30 a.m. Wander around for a while and try not to wake anyone up. Browse the bookshelf and pick a few books to thumb through. I can always depend on Matt to turn me on to a good book. The dude reads everything.
- 8:00 a.m. Everyone is up. We eat migas and beans while the coffee works its way through everyone's veins.
- 8:15 a.m. Turn on the TV. Flip through the news channels and get mad at the talking heads. Flip to the Weather Channel and start compulsively watching the radar. Jim Cantore is about to get smacked around by the storm. You don't want to be near Jim when a hurricane is bearing down.
- 10:00 a.m. Talk about life stuff with Matt and Laura. Regardless of the circumstances, it's good to see them again.
- 1:00 p.m. Watch one of the six movies we picked up at the movie store.
- 3:00 p.m. Flip to the Weather Channel again. Worry about finishing the trip in time for school.
- 3:30 p.m. Think about taking a shower. Decide it can wait.
- 4:00 p.m. Watch another movie.
- 7:30 p.m. Go into Oxford and see the sights. What a neat little town. They have a lot of beer there.
- 9:30 p.m. Start the last movie. Sleep off and on during it.

- 12:00 a.m. Go on the porch and figure out the world's problems with Matt.
- 2:00 a.m. Lie down on the air mattress. Repeat the process the next day.

It's been a great visit, but I'm getting super edgy about all this weather. There have been four named hurricanes already, and we're barely into the season. Once we get back on the water, we're on our own, as we don't know anyone else downriver. Logistics will get interesting in a hurry if we have to bail again because of the weather.

Harold, our computerized weather radio guy, gives us the local weather, but we need to know what's happening in the Gulf of Mexico, some four hundred miles away.

The more we wait, the faster the clock ticks.

Tick.
Tick.
Tick.

Watching the radar all day is driving me nuts. We need to get back on the river before I lose my damn mind.

We're *this* close to finishing, but man, it's gonna be tight.

MEMPHIS BLUES
MEMPHIS, TENNESSEE - MILE 1,565

We're heading back to the river after spending three days hiding from a hurricane. The Memphis Yacht Club let us store the canoe here for free while the storm blew through. The outpouring of support humbles me. We've have a lot of karma to pay forward. Thanks, y'all.

I'm sure we've gotten a little soft. I expect to find a few muscles that atrophied while sitting on the couch and eating stupid amounts of food, but it's time to head downstream. Being out of the canoe has made us edgy, and we're both ready to get back into the groove. We have just over two weeks to finish the trip, so every day counts.

There's a massive amount of water flushing down the river, and I'm anxious to see how this plays out. Even with the time off, we're still on track to finish by the end of July. August 1 is our cutoff—just enough time to rest, unpack, and head back to class. Being crunched for time sucks, but it is what it is.

Tropical Storm Emily might be headed our way soon. Our options if the weather gets too dangerous are (a) getting off and waiting a few more days (time permitting), (b) getting off and going home, or (c) taking the Atchafalaya River down to the Gulf of Mexico.

We have to make that decision this week before we get to the Atchafalaya, but for now, we're just watching the skies and figuring it out as we go.

Left to its own devices, the Mississippi would pour into the Atchafalaya Basin instead of heading to New Orleans. Even now, the Atchafalaya already takes about 30% of the flow from the Mississippi. There are several historical and economic reasons why the river continues to flow to New Orleans. The levees, wing dams, and locks constructed by the Corps of Engineers are doing their best to keep the Mississippi in check, for now. I've got a feeling that Mama Nature will have the final word in the end.

So here we are, ready to put in. One hurricane just blew through, and another is probably on the way. The river might not cooperate with our plan, or any backup plan, for that matter. At this point, we're just playing it day by day and hoping for the best. We've paddled for two months to get here and would love to see it through. Rain, we can handle. Hurricanes? That's another thing entirely. Some things are just out of our control.

July 12, 2005

TWENTY YEARS LATER...

Okay, I'm not gonna lie. Getting back on the river in Memphis was scary. Like, *scary*, scary. It damn near derailed the whole trip.

Looking back, we should have waited one more day. Barge traffic had stopped for several days, and this was the first day they were back on the river en masse. Barges and tows were everywhere, and a massive amount of water was flushing down from the Missouri, Ohio, and Upper Mississippi rivers. Combine that with tons of trash, trees popping up out of the water from out of nowhere, wild currents, and other floating weirdness, and all that made things way, way too interesting for me.

The river spit us back whenever we tried to get off the shore and into the current. We finally got off the water, made a bunch of phone calls, walked around, and ate snacks. Truth be told, it was mostly Jess talking me down off the ledge. I was scared and ready to bail.

A couple of hours later, we had one of the best afternoons of paddling of the entire trip and camped on a five-star sandbar. Go figure.

But for a while there...*damn.*

BRIDGES AND DAMS

I love bridges. Always have.

When we started way up north, the bridges were tiny— just a few feet above the water. One of the first ones was the Richard Felt Bridge near the headwaters. It was barely four feet high, so we ducked and glided through with just a little room to spare.

The farther south we go, the bigger the bridges get. I love seeing how they're built—the girders, the beams, the pilings. Sometimes, as we pass beneath them, barn swallows burst out of their nests and circle around us. We hear them peeping in the distance before they swoop back home. Other times, they just peek out from their mud huts and watch us float by.

Bridges mark time. They're fixed points showing you exactly where you are, how many miles you've

Richard Felt Bridge, MN

done, and how many you still have to go. We've had people wave at us, stare at us, or ignore us completely. Just two tiny people in a tiny canoe, a hundred feet below.

We saw Memphis's distinctive "M" bridge from miles away. It took over an hour to get there. Sometimes the river makes you earn your landmarks.

Bridges give shelter. The sun. The rain. The heat. When you're paddling along, the person in front gets their shade first. The one in back has to keep paddling until relief finally hits them. Three seconds of pure envy. We hid from thunderstorms in Minneapolis and ducked into the shade under tons more since then. In more ways than one, bridges have been our protectors.

Hiding from the rain

We've paddled beneath bridges jammed with bumper-to-bumper traffic, and all I could think was, *I'm glad I'm down here on the river instead of stuck in that mess.*

Anytime we're home and drive across a bridge over a river, we slow down a little. We lean toward the window, look down, and ask the same question.

"I wonder where that river goes?"

Yeah. I love bridges.

The Mississippi isn't just spanned by bridges. It's hemmed in, slowed down, and chopped into pieces by over 40 dams along the way. In the headwaters between Lake Itasca and Bemidji, the first dams are natural. Lots of beaver dams and fallen trees for us to scramble over or around. From Bemidji to Minneapolis, there are about a dozen man-made dams, some of them set up in the late 1800s to power flour mills, sawmills, and to provide some measure of flood control. Between Minneapolis and St Louis, there are twenty-nine locks and dams, each one built to tame the river for barges, navigation, and industry.

Blanchard Dam, Minnesota

For us, every dam means two things: a portage and a pool. Behind each dam sits a stretch of slow-moving water that feels like paddling through maple syrup. You don't get any free miles in those pools, and you don't want to get stuck in the middle of one with the wind pipes up and the waves get going.

Below Minneapolis, you can run through the locks, but sometimes it's not worth the wait. We would rather shoulder the canoe and cut around than sit for hours while barges lock through. Either way, the river makes you pay. Sometimes it's a paved ramp, sometimes it's a muddy scramble through weeds. As always, portaging builds character.

July 14, 2005

IN ROBERT JOHNSON'S FOOTSTEPS
FRIARS POINT, MISSISSIPPI

Our trusty gas station map, which we'd been using for hundreds of miles, doesn't give much detail about the river, especially when it comes to docks and landing locations. You were on your own to guess where the towns were. Most of the time, you can't even see towns over the levees, so you just take your best shot.

Our GPS insisted we were three miles inland and wasn't much help either.

"Look, dude, I told you. We're on the river right now. We're floating in the damn canoe. What. About. That. Do. You. Not. Understand?"

Stupid GPS.

We were running low on water, so we decided to stop in Friars Point to pick up a couple of gallons, upload a story to the newspaper, and check email—quick in and out, right?

We thought we were close when we spotted a small landing. We tied up the canoe and hiked up the levee, assuming the town was just over the top.

We got to the top and found nothing but a road running through a string of cow pastures. It had to be just a little farther, right?

That "little farther" turned into a two-mile hike. No matter. The road was good, and we didn't get gored by any bulls. They just stood there chewing their cud as you do.

It was a beautiful day anyway. A good day for a hike.

After about an hour, we finally made it to town. Before the Civil War, Friars Point was the biggest cotton port south of Memphis. Now it's a shell of that booming past.

Shotgun blasts through doorways, broken windows, and boarded-up houses. We passed homes with barking dogs chained in the yard. We hung a left at the Mississippi Limestone ramp by the factory. That's where we should have landed in the first place. But hey, nice day and all.

Robert Johnson name-dropped Friars Point in 'Traveling Riverside Blues.' Not much is known about Johnson, but Muddy Waters once watched him play in front of Hirsberg's Drugstore here in town. He walked away after a while, calling Johnson a "dangerous man." Johnson died at 27, likely poisoned by an irate husband. His name would eventually join the ranks of the "27 Club," which includes Jimi Hendrix, Keith Moon, Janis Joplin, Kurt Cobain, and Jean-Michel Basquiat.

We asked around and eventually found the Community Resource Center a few blocks away. Inside was a room with a dozen computers, job-hunting guides, and a mix of folks—some kids doing schoolwork and a couple of dudes playing video games.

Places like this are absolute lifelines for rural kids. It reminded me of the big blue bookmobile that used to stop at the Climax General Store. I'd check out a grocery bag full of books and disappear into my room for two weeks. It was also where I learned about library fines. I've paid hundreds of dollars in late fees over the years, and they've been worth every penny.

Anyway, I knocked out our newspaper story, Jess uploaded some photos, we hit the bathroom, grabbed our water, and headed back out of town.

Back past the churches, the houses, and the dogs. Back to our levee road and our two-mile hike to the canoe.

It was a beautiful day for a walk, and we were thankful to be there.

Friar's Point Levee Walk

LIFE BETWEEN THE LEVEES

The U.S. Army Corps of Engineers have built a levee system to control flooding and maintain a navigable channel down the Mississippi. We started seeing them well above St. Louis and have been inside ever since. It's a whole different world inside the levees.

Towns are invisible, save for the occasional water tower or grain elevator peeking over the levees. Recreational boat traffic has all but disappeared. The desolation is so relentless that it feels personal.

Mark Twain, quoting Captain Marryat, RN, described this stretch in *Life on the Mississippi*.

"There are no pleasing associations connected with the great common sewer of the Western America, which pours out its mud into the Mexican Gulf, polluting the clear blue sea for many miles beyond its mouth. It is a river of desolation; and instead of reminding you, like other beautiful rivers, of an angel which has descended for the benefit of man, you imagine it a devil, whose energies have been only overcome by the wonderful power of steam."

I wouldn't go that far, but I get it. The contrast is stark. Fewer birds. Fewer fish. More sandbars. More Silence. But there's something calming about the emptiness. No towns, no traffic. Just us and the river. The afternoons are hot, hazy, and suffocating, but there are miles of sandbars to explore. We're on our own now, more aware than ever that we have to watch out for ourselves.

Taking a break

THE CROSSROADS
VICKSBURG, MISSISSIPPI - MILE 1,866

We had a moment of reflection a few days ago after encountering really weird currents near a wing dam while a barge wake was bearing down on us at the same time. They combined, resulting in a nasty whirlpool ON THE SIDE OF THE DAMN WAVE that we had to paddle through.

To paraphrase the conversation, it went something like, *"Goodness! What an interesting situation we are encountering!"*

The actual conversation was much shorter, and much *louder*.

We finally made it to Vicksburg yesterday. This has been by far the hardest week of the trip.

When we left Memphis, we knew Hurricane Emily was in the Gulf of Mexico, but didn't know where she was heading. Our weather radio doesn't provide forecasts more than 50 miles away, but we've been getting weather updates all week from friends and family whenever we can get a cell phone signal.

Our weather worries have subsided a little, and we're in the home stretch. I can't believe we've already had so many hurricanes and tropical storms this year. Don't want to jinx anything, but we should finish in about a week if the weather holds off. *(Note: 2005 would be a record-breaking year for storms. 27 named storms and 14 hurricanes, including hurricanes Katrina and Rita.)*

A thunderstorm blew in just as we reached the confluence of the Yazoo and Mississippi rivers near Vicksburg. We couldn't paddle up the Yazoo in that mess, so we hid the canoe behind an abandoned barge and hiked toward town. It wasn't the best place to hide the canoe, but we planned to pick it up after a quick trip to the post office for our mail drop.

That quick hike turned out to be a few miles. It was far enough that we didn't want to return to the canoe, so we only had the clothes on our backs and a small bag of personal gear when we got to the post office.

We walked downtown to the visitor's center and asked about motels. The lady gave us the name of the casino and another, more economical, motel up the street. When I asked about a cheaper place, she replied, *"Well, honey, you'll just have to see it yourself."*

We got the hint and didn't need much convincing to hit the all-you-can-eat buffet at the casino. The buffet was amazing, and Jess won enough playing the slot machine to pay for the night!

We smelled bad, like Something-the-Dog-Rolled-In-Bad. The accumulation of a week's worth of sweat, sunscreen, sand, and funk made for a tidal wave of odor. We washed our clothes in the bathtub and left a ring of mud four inches high. I may need to burn my shorts.

We're in the Mississippi Audubon Society's district office discussing our trip and ways to help further their work. We're happy to be associated with Audubon and believe in their programs to protect the river and its habitats. The staff here has been kind enough to give us the lay of the land and open up their office for us to use.

Vicksburg was hopping today. We toured a new art park that was nearing completion on the riverfront. The park is based on the steamer The *Sprague*. At 318 feet long, the *Sprague* was the largest and most powerful sternwheeler towboat ever built. Kids were already all over the playground, and it'll be a great addition to the riverfront area.

Catfish Row Children's Art Park, Vicksburg, MS

Assuming our canoe and gear are still hidden in the bushes, we'll be back on the water this afternoon. It's been hard to tear ourselves out of town, but the river is calling, and there are about 300 more miles to go.

July 19, 2005

UNPLUGGING

"Unplugging is one of the things I'm looking forward to most. I'm sure the economy, war, Michael Jackson, Tom DeLay, the NBA, imports, exports, school boards, evolution, devolution, summer blockbusters, Brad and Jen, Angelina, Britney's baby, and any number of worldly events will get along fine without me for a while. I'm information overloaded, and I need to throw a few things overboard." - May 8, 2005

I found that little gem the other day while flipping through my journal. Before we left, I spent hours every day just doing 'stuff.' Life 'stuff.' School 'stuff.' Wasting time 'stuff.'

We're bombarded every day with mountains of garbage. Something always comes at you from when you wake up until you nod off. Turn off the alarm and turn on the radio. Listen to the talking heads blather about the drama of the day. Billboards everywhere. TV shows that do nothing but melt your brain. The drivel on somebody's blog, eating up time and energy. All this crap is just a distraction, and I'm as sucked into it as the next guy. I was ready to unplug.

We spend countless hours just enjoying each other's company.

Being in the moment all the time is just what the doctor ordered. I've got to remember to stay out of those old ruts when we get back home. I don't need to be Siddhartha sitting under a banyan tree to be happy, but I don't need to be hip-deep in the world's mire either.

Vicksburg Shopping List
A Little of This, a Little of That

I dug this shopping list out of my dry bag the other day, and I'm glad I kept it. It's nothing groundbreaking, but the mundane stuff brings back the most memories for me. I bet we've sent back a Rubbermaid tub full of maps, brochures, magazines, and all that kind of stuff, but little scraps of paper like this shopping list are like time capsules to be opened up later.

Let's see, we made this list at the Horizon Casino in Vicksburg. We needed to grab a few things on the way back to the canoe. Super-glue, bread, peanut butter, squeeze cheese, Velveeta, and dainty wipes. Yeah, that's what's on the menu.

At this point, my flip phone is held together with duct tape, paper clips, hot glue, and unreasonable optimism. For my next trick, I'm gonna try super-gluing some zip ties and a scrap of nylon to hold it together better. I'm sure that's going to work *just fine.*

We've been living on sandwiches and snack foods for about a week. There's plenty of room in the 5-gallon food buckets, so the bread doesn't get squashed. The ham's for the first few sandwiches out of town. We're not carrying a cooler, and honestly, we don't miss it. It's just more stuff to drag around.

We got hooked on this Nestlé latte mix back in Minnesota and try to track it down in every town. It mixes great with the dried milk we use, and it's tasty, tasty, tasty. Come to think of it, we haven't made actual coffee on this trip at all.

The "Tango" is just some generic orange drink mix that adds a little flavor to our blood-temperature water. Velveeta, squeeze cheese, crackers, and snacks. *The Lunch of Champions!*

Dainty wipes? That's just our nickname for baby wipes, and baby wipes are essential.

I love that we can take some fresh stuff with us. Carrots, crackers, hummus, some apples, and a chunk of cheese? I could live on that.

Dainty wipes, squeeze cheese, and two tubes of superglue? Somebody could have a good weekend with a list like that.

Tucking this list away and heading down the river.

Onward, with squeeze cheese

Super glue (2)

Bread (2)
Peanut butter
water (gallon)
squeeze cheese
velvetta

Rice dinner
ham or something for sandwiches
crackers
Tango
Latte or hot choc
snacks

carrots
peaches

daintywipes

DRINKING WATER
THE GIARDIA™ WEIGHT-LOSS PLAN

For the first two weeks, most of our drinking water came from the river. We were careful to treat everything, since that area has plenty of beavers and other critters, increasing the possibility of contracting giardia. Giardiasis is a serious illness caused by ingesting some flagellated protozoa affectionately named Giardia duodenalis. What happens is you ingest the protozoa, then they hang out in your small intestine for a few weeks. Soon, the Giardia cysts start partying together, and then that partying begets more protozoa swimming around. A microscopic, intestinal rave. Once that process is in full force, it's game over. Closest exit wins.

Giardiasis involves weeks of nausea and constant sprints to the bathroom. I contracted this delightful malady about ten years ago and still cringe thinking about it. Three weeks, some awful meds, and twenty-five pounds later, it had run its course. I wouldn't wish it on anyone. Ok, almost anyone.

Water in the northern stretch was easy to obtain from the marinas and towns. Down here, the towns are few and far between, leaving us longer hikes with the water jugs. We left Memphis with almost fourteen gallons of water, and at eight pounds per gallon, that's over one hundred pounds of extra weight to lug around. It's worth every ounce. We ran out of water once right after St. Louis, but once was enough.

And just because I've always got something stupid spinning around in my head, here's my infomercial script for **The GIARDIA™ Weight-Loss Plan.**

Coming Soon: GIARDIA™
The Weight-Loss Plan That Really Moves You

Would you like to lose 10, 20, or 30 pounds quickly and easily?
Harness the ancient power of GIARDIA™! Guaranteed results for
today's sedentary lifestyle.
No working out!
No special diet!
Just fast, easy results.

Why waste time away from your television to lose weight? Our
patented *Protozoan Colon Cleansing System* will give you the slim
figure you desire without leaving the bathroom!
Order your GIARDIA™ Weight-Loss Plan today!

GIARDIA™
It's what's inside you that counts.

Natchez, Mississippi

MILE 1,947

"*Hey, you can't park that thing here!*" was the call welcoming us to Natchez.

I asked the security guy at the Isle of Capri Casino if we could tie up nearby. He wouldn't give me a straight answer, so I asked to speak to the captain. After he conferred with who I'm guessing was the captain, cook, steward, garbage man, and chief brass shiner, we got permission to land near their floating house of cards. Being in a sour mood, I tied the canoe six inches past their property line.

I smell like roadkill and feel like death. Lately, I've been stressing about how we can finish up before another hurricane comes or we run out of money. It's been a great trip, but all good things must come to an end. Better to leave before the magic wears off than to drag things out much longer.

I'm looking forward to the Atchafalaya. Everyone we've talked to says it's fantastic. Tons of bayous, swamps, gators, and more birds. Now *that's* the way to end this trip.

"HONEY, I LOVE YOU, BUT PLEASE STOP BREATHING"

It's been hotter than Satan's butt crack. Highs have been over 100 degrees all week, and the forecast calls for more of the same. The rubber case on the binoculars melted off the other day, and setting up the tent on hot sand creates a perfect portable sauna. All the heat is trapped inside, and we lie there, buck naked, praying for the faintest puff of wind to cool things off. I'm absolutely smoked. I feel like I say that all the time, but really, it's pretty damn hot.

You could fry an egg on the canoe right now. Sunny side up.

I'm convinced I'm going to spontaneously combust like a *Spinal Tap* drummer soon.

July 21, 2005

"THE ITINERARY"
THE CRUELEST TASKMASTER

This damn thing. The Despot of Despair. Harbinger of Heartache. Barometer of Bullshit.

"The Itinerary."

I've carried this stupid thing the whole way and looked at it a million times. Math scribbles are all over it. All division. No multiplication. Just subtraction of time.

The Equation

Number of Miles ÷ X Days =?

A spike in stress?

Calm reflection on how far we've come?

None of the above?

I cooked up this stupid torture chamber after reading every book, article, or website of anyone who'd paddled this thing I could get my hands on. Bruce "Buck" Nelson took 67 days, solo. He did his trip immediately after thru-hiking the Appalachian Trail. As in, he hiked 2,150 miles on the AT, then two weeks later started down the Mississippi River. Bruce lives a big life. He's a smokejumper in Alaska, thru-hiked all the major trails, climbed big-name mountains (Kilimanjaro, Aconcagua, etc), and has done a ton of other stuff I'm forgetting.

Nice guy. Emailed him before our trip with questions that I'm sure he's answered a million times. He's just a total beast.

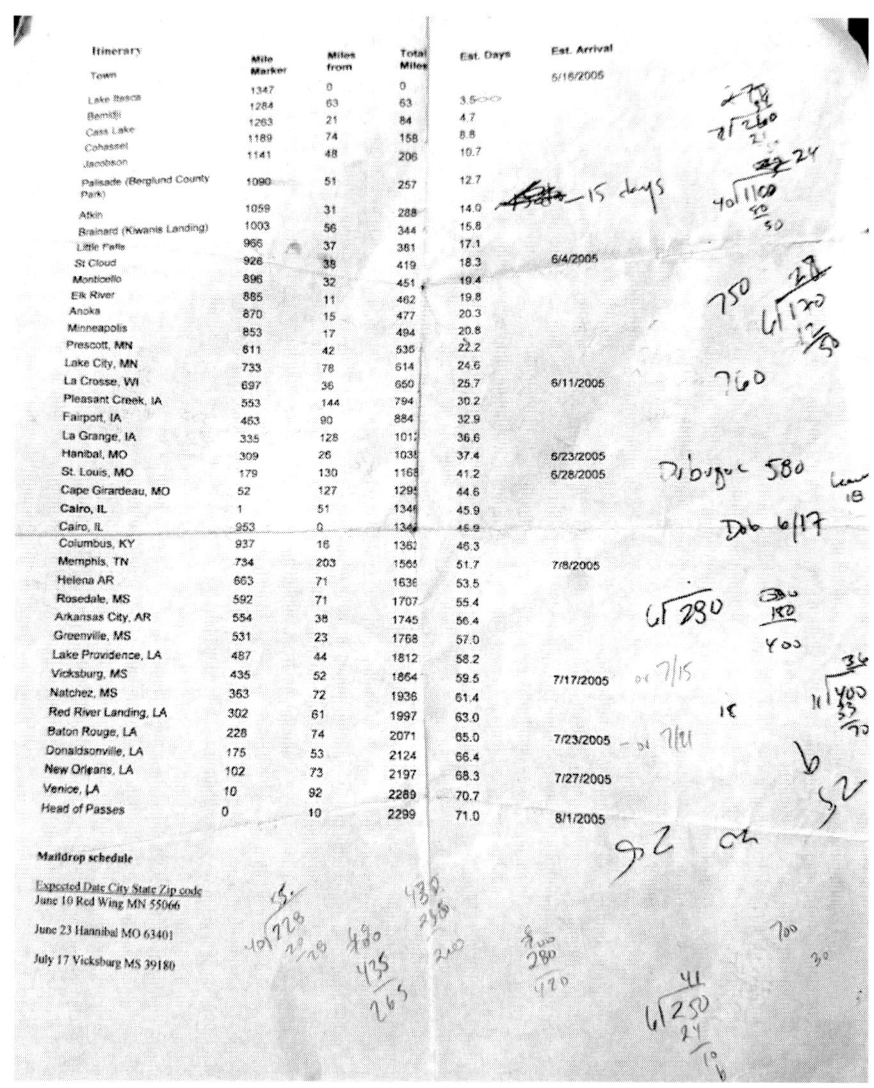

Itinerary Town	Mile Marker	Miles from	Total Miles	Est. Days	Est. Arrival 5/16/2005
Lake Itasca	1347	0	0		
Bemidji	1284	63	63	3.5	
Cass Lake	1263	21	84	4.7	
Cohasset	1189	74	158	8.8	
Jacobson	1141	48	206	10.7	
Palisade (Berglund County Park)	1090	51	257	12.7	
Atkin	1059	31	288	14.0	
Brainard (Kiwanis Landing)	1003	56	344	15.8	
Little Falls	966	37	381	17.1	
St Cloud	928	38	419	18.3	6/4/2005
Monticello	896	32	451	19.4	
Elk River	885	11	462	19.8	
Anoka	870	15	477	20.3	
Minneapolis	853	17	494	20.8	
Prescott, MN	811	42	536	22.2	
Lake City, MN	733	78	614	24.6	
La Crosse, WI	697	36	650	25.7	6/11/2005
Pleasant Creek, IA	553	144	794	30.2	
Fairport, IA	463	90	884	32.9	
La Grange, IA	335	128	1012	36.6	
Hanibal, MO	309	26	1038	37.4	6/23/2005
St. Louis, MO	179	130	1168	41.2	6/28/2005
Cape Girardeau, MO	52	127	1295	44.6	
Cairo, IL	1	51	1346	45.9	
Cairo, IL	953	0	1346	45.9	
Columbus, KY	937	16	1362	46.3	
Memphis, TN	734	203	1565	51.7	7/8/2005
Helena AR	663	71	1636	53.5	
Rosedale, MS	592	71	1707	55.4	
Arkansas City, AR	554	38	1745	56.4	
Greenville, MS	531	23	1768	57.0	
Lake Providence, LA	487	44	1812	58.2	
Vicksburg, MS	435	52	1864	59.5	7/17/2005
Natchez, MS	363	72	1936	61.4	
Red River Landing, LA	302	61	1997	63.0	
Baton Rouge, LA	228	74	2071	65.0	7/23/2005
Donaldsonville, LA	175	53	2124	66.4	
New Orleans, LA	102	73	2197	68.3	7/27/2005
Venice, LA	10	92	2289	70.7	
Head of Passes	0	10	2299	71.0	8/1/2005

Maildrop schedule

Expected Date City State Zip code
June 10 Red Wing MN 55066

June 23 Hannibal MO 63401

July 17 Vicksburg MS 39180

Mississippi River Itinerary

ALBERT TOUSLEY PADDLED his wood-and-canvas canoe the full length in 1925, in 105 days. He's generally considered the first to do it. I loved his book, *Where Goes the River.*

Guy Haglund took 101 days.

Verlen Kruger and Bob Bradford took 24 days. Verlen was 79 at the time. Holy shit.

Note to self: be more like Verlen.

Anyway, I took copious notes of everything and started on this spreadsheet from hell. I guesstimated we had about 80 days at most between the spring and fall semesters. Took off a few days, carried the 1, waved a wet finger in the wind, and started pulling numbers out of my butt.

Looking at it, we're pretty close to where we thought we'd be. Neither Jess nor I like to screw around much in camp and would rather be in the canoe than anywhere else. I bet we'd be in the same place even if we didn't have this schedule breathing down our necks the whole time. Ideally, we'd have an open-ended date, but it is what it is.

In any case, the weather this year has been beyond weird. Lots of named storms already, including the hurricane we just dodged. I can't help but think that the next storm has our number. We just need to finish before it catches up to us.

POSTSCRIPT: *Hurricane Katrina made landfall four weeks after we finished.*

ATCHAFALAYA RIVER
THE ROAD LESS TRAVELED

I shall be telling this with a sigh
Somewhere ages and ages hence:
Two roads diverged in a wood, and I—
I took the one less traveled by,
And that has made all the difference.
-Robert Frost

OLD RIVER CONTROL STRUCTURE, MILE 1,994

We started the trip knowing we could go down the Atchafalaya River to the Gulf of Mexico if we wanted to. The closer we got, the more the conversation turned to which river to take. Stick with the Mississippi and not see another soul for the rest of the trip? Maybe. The lower Mississippi felt more like a giant ditch—just sandbars, levees, and barges as far as we could see. On the other hand, seeing New Orleans and paddling 100 more miles to Mile Marker Zero would give a great sense of continuity. Think 2-lane blacktop vs. taking the interstate.

The Atchafalaya has its own challenges, starting with the fact that we had no information on it. Maps for both the lower Mississippi and the Atchafalaya are scarce. I'd been hunting for the Lower Mississippi set for weeks. The Corps of Engineers were reprinting them this year, and nobody seemed to know where to find a copy. I'd ordered months ago, but nothing ever showed. So for hundreds of miles, we've been navigating with nothing more than a gas station highway map.

Life Jacket Tanline

Folks we talked to upstream told us stories of bayous and alligators on the Atchafalaya. The Mississippi and Atchafalaya rivers run roughly parallel for a while before the Mississippi flows southeast toward Baton Rouge and New Orleans. The Atchafalaya is at the same or lower elevation as the Mississippi. Folks speculate that without the levees and flood controls, the Mississippi would fill with silt, hop its banks, and flow down the Atchafalaya basin.

A tremendous amount of resources and infrastructure have been built to ensure the Mississippi ends up in New Orleans, but I've got to wonder how long that will last. One hundred years? A thousand? The New Madrid earthquake of 1812 is the largest earthquake to hit the lower 48 states and caused the river to wildly change its path around the New Madrid fault. According to eyewitnesses, the river reversed course and flowed north for a while. The dynamic forces of nature tend to mock our best efforts to control them.

Bruce Reed and Tom Pullen from the Audubon Society's office in Vicksburg were a great resource in deciding which way to go. Both men knew the Atchafalaya well and came through with a few maps and some much-needed advice. Ultimately, we decided to take the road less traveled.

Once past the Old River Control Structure (*and if that's not the greatest name for a government facility, I don't know what is*), we turned right toward the lock that would take us to the Atchafalaya. Looking back at the Mississippi as we veered off, I couldn't help but wonder what paddling through Baton Rouge and New Orleans would have been like.

We've paddled the Mississippi for 2,000 miles, watching it grow from a tiny creek into a massive river. It's hard not to feel a bit nostalgic stepping away now. It's weird. But the Atchafalaya promises its own surprises, and I'm excited for what's ahead. It's a new river, a new vibe, and the Gulf is getting closer.

LATER THAT DAY...

Man, this is one cool river! What a massive difference in scenery and paddling. We knew this was the right decision for us as soon as we got through the lock. So many things to see! More birds, fish, and other wildlife. We saw the first fishermen in weeks and had a beer. It's almost the complete opposite of what the Mississippi was.

We'd planned to get water at the lock but couldn't find a way in. Barbed wire fencing, chained gates—everything locked down like a prison. We walked all the way around to the locked front gate. I found an intercom and finally got in touch with someone to let us through.

I went to the lockmaster's office and was greeted at the door. *"Good afternoon, John."*

That threw me for a second. I hadn't told him my name. Turns out the lockmaster had zoomed in on our canoe, saw **www.-source2sea.info** plastered on the side, and was flipping through the website by the time I'd made it around.

John the Lock Guy (lots of Johns in this world) took us under his wing and tried to give us the shirt off his back. Within five minutes, he had offered us the use of his truck and a place to stay. I felt awful turning him down, but we were finally in the home stretch and itching to see this new river. His generosity was greatly appreciated though. Another benevolent stranger came into our lives from out of the blue, and I hope to return the favor sometime.

July 22, 2005

BUTTERFLIES AND SWIMMING LOGS

Today was one of those magical, fairy-tale river days.

We stopped to have our late lunch, as usual. While we were cooking, a bunch of butterflies flew closer and closer. They finally landed on us to sip the salt off our arms. It was so calm and so chill. I live for that kind of stuff.

After we set up camp, I decided to wash off in the river. I was about knee-deep when I watched a small log float downstream. No big deal. Washed off some more, and then that small log started swimming upstream. Real slow. Real deliberate. I got out before that small log decided to take a chomp out of me.

This right here is my jam. Man, I freaking love the Atchafalaya.

Atchafalaya River Lunch Stop

THE DEAD ZONE AND ASIAN CARP

I'd read about the Dead Zone before we left, but after about 2000 miles of paddling, we've seen it up close and personal. The silt load entering the river is enormous, as is the amount of pollution that gets dumped in. Nitrogen and phosphorus from farm runoff eventually make their way downriver into the Gulf of Mexico. These extra nutrients feed the algae to unsustainable levels, blocking sunlight that would usually reach the seafloor.

As the algae die off and decompose, they consume much of the dissolved oxygen in the water, making it uninhabitable for plant and animal life. This process, called *eutrophication,* has severely impacted the fishing industry and tourism, among other things. The area seriously affected in the Gulf is called the Dead Zone, and last year it covered over 6,000 square miles.

The Dead Zone is a seasonal occurrence that continues to grow each summer, year after year, causing significant harm to the delicate marine ecosystem. What happens in Minnesota, or Iowa, or any of the 32 states and 2 Canadian provinces, doesn't stay there. That's a hell of a legacy for America's greatest river.

Asian carp are an invasive species wreaking havoc on the ecosystems of the Mississippi, Missouri, and Illinois rivers. They can out-eat and out-spawn all the native species, crowding everything else out. They don't reach nearly that size back overseas, but the warm water and lack of fishing pressure make these carp the kudzu of the river.

We've heard stories about Asian carp knocking people out of their boats. There have been a few serious injuries from silver and bighead carp flying out of the water when a boat goes by. It's not unusual for these beasts to reach seventy pounds or more and jump twenty feet through the air. If it's all the same, I'd prefer to keep my distance from those things.

Funky water on the Mississippi

ALMOST HOME

MILE 2,099

Today was brutal, but we're almost home. Spent the night on the only patch of dryish land we'd seen for miles. We stumbled out of the tent and were on the river by 4:30 a.m. to make some big miles before dark. From what we could tell, Hurricane Emily was blowing out to Mexico, but we have no idea what's behind her. It'd be nice to have better weather information, but we have what we have.

A chill was in the air when we pushed off this morning. Sunrise wasn't due for another hour, so Jess bundled up and slept in the bow while I paddled in the stern. Most days, I just see the back of her head as we ramble on about one thing or another, but this morning, we didn't speak a word once we shoved off.

There's little development down this way, and having the river to ourselves is relaxing. The river was dead calm, and the only sound was the splash of our paddles and the occasional fish jumping out of the water.

The afternoons have been scorching, but it'd be too much to ask for an early frost this time of year. Getting off the water at 2 p.m. is frustrating because we want to keep paddling, but the heat is so intense that you feel like you're going to melt. A dull haze covers everything by the middle of the day, and neither man nor beast comes out until it cools off.

We covered about fifty-five miles today and should reach Morgan City tomorrow afternoon. We'll need to finalize the arrangements for our ride home, and then, one last push to the Gulf.

I'm having a hard time getting my head around the idea that we're almost done. It's so surreal. Watching a little creek grow into this astounding river has been amazing. I'm blessed to have shared it with Jess.

No matter what, the Mississippi and Atchafalaya rivers are tattooed to our souls.

July 25, 2005

IT IS DONE
MORGAN CITY, LOUISIANA - MILE 2,152

So many emotions and memories are swirling through my head right now, I don't know where to start. I'm a sobbing, sunburned, sloppy mess, so I'll just start here, in Morgan City, after 2,152 miles and 73 days on the river.

The last few days have been some of the best of the trip so far. Hot, to be sure, but great all the same. We struggled with the decision to take the Atchafalaya River to the Gulf instead of the Mississippi, but it worked out great for us. We met more locals this way, and the smaller river allowed us to spend more time reflecting and less time dodging barges. Ultimately, taking the road less traveled proved to be far better for us. Highly recommended.

Yesterday afternoon, we sat out a monster thunderstorm in Morgan City's town pavilion for a few hours as lightning crashed around us. We spent last night in a soaking-wet tent, in a mud puddle, on a mosquito-infested sandbar just a few inches above the waterline. It didn't matter at all. I'm just glad to have made it here without any injuries or major incidents. There's some lingering soreness, a slight sunburn, and tender hands, but nothing else of consequence.

193

Abandoned boats on Atchafalaya River

Everything seems like a dream. Looking through some of the photos, I feel worlds away from Minnesota and everything in between. It's...weird.

We've been dodging hurricanes and storms for the past month but wanted to get as close to the Gulf of Mexico as possible. Once past Morgan City, there is nothing but swamps, and you're committed to being on the water.

Some locals told us about a sandbar that would be our only chance of finding a place to camp. We planned to paddle about fifteen miles past Morgan City and camp, then return the following day through Bayou Shaffer and the Intracoastal Waterway after seeing the Gulf.

The sandbar was only about four inches above the high waterline. We pulled the canoe up as far as we could and tied it to a downed log, hoping the water wouldn't rise too much.

The sandbar was like quicksand, but we set up the tent in the best place possible. Didn't bother with a sleeping bag because it was still ninety degrees. Nighttime was approaching, and we could hear the mosquitoes getting restless in the swamp behind our little oasis. There was no other place in the world we'd rather be.

Water leaked through every seam as the tent slowly sank into the mud. It didn't matter. It took 73 days to get there, and we couldn't be happier. We started at a creek and found an ocean.

We made it.

We are officially River Rats.

And it feels awesome.

July 27, 2005

End of the Source to Sea Expedition. Mile 2,152. Morgan City, LA

Last Sunset on the Atchafalaya River

EPILOGUE

Well, we did it. I still can't believe it. Our buddy Amanda came down to pick us up in Morgan City, and from there we headed to New Orleans for a photo shoot with the Audubon Society. That night, we made good on the promise we'd made to the lockmaster in Minneapolis—we went to Pat O'Brien's and drank hurricanes until our tongues turned red.

Amanda and Jess wisely called it a night, while I unwisely chose to trade shots with some Irish dudes for the next couple of hours, an ill-conceived plan at best. I somehow made it back to our hotel and ended up in the bathtub, room spinning, hoping and praying for some benevolent being to strike me down where I lay. Sorry, ladies.

The Mississippi River trip was audacious, unpredictable, ridiculously challenging, and I loved it all, even the parts that scared the crap out of me. I especially loved sharing it with Jess. She's unflappable, funny, and super smart. I do love her so. Going down the river with her means the world to me.

We got married in 2007 and have settled down in Raleigh, NC. We have a house, two kids, fulfilling careers, the whole bit. We adopted a dog about a year ago. I'm not sure who really rescued whom, but Bingo the Dog-O is the best boy.

We're a tight-knit family and love being involved with our schools, PTA, music, drama, sports, and more. I've done some weird stuff in my life, but being a dad is by far the weirdest thing ever, and it's awesome. I love being a dad to our two boys.

Like most parents, we try to introduce our kids to opportunities we didn't have and show them that there's a big world out there. Teaching them to be good humans, appreciate the outdoors, and the importance of giving a damn. The value of dreaming big, coming up with a plan, and going for it. We're not perfect, but I'd like to think that we've had more wins than losses in this department.

We took both boys out for their first paddling trips when they were about 6 months old. Though we've both paddled thousands of miles and were on a calm river less than 8 inches deep, we had about six different emergency plans in place and were mildly terrified. The boys slept through it all, and I'm glad we got them set off on the road to perdition and paddling early.

About two years after we finished, Jess developed cataracts and needed eye surgery. From that came two detached retinas and some more scary procedures. She was effectively blind for about two years but came through it with flying colors and now has excellent vision.

Jess has worked with nonprofits, including the Neuse River-keeper Foundation and EarthShare North Carolina. She now works for the state of North Carolina, kicking butt and taking names as she does. Currently working to help get broadband internet access to underserved areas.

When we got off the water, I felt like I could do anything. I was physically strong but emotionally still a bit of a mess. I had a lot of things hanging over my head, and, as I've said a million times before, long trips like that are both the best and the worst place to try to work it all out.

I made it one more year before I flamed out of my PhD. I then worked for the university for five years before falling backward into my current career. I was playing gigs around town using a home-made three-string guitar. I made it from an old Frito-Lay lunchbox I had when I was a kid, now known as the "Fritocaster." I thought to myself, "Hey, I should probably make some merch."

I made five shirts, sold them, made ten more, and went from there. I planned to do that for about two years. That was 15 years ago. The company is called House of Swank, and we've since evolved into an experiential marketing company. We do a fair amount of e-commerce and wholesale, but primarily host live screen printing events for conventions, conferences, and similar events. You can find us at **www.HouseofSwankClothing.com.**

I still use much of the gear we took down the river. My PFD always brings back fond memories, although it somehow shrank in the closet over the years. Weird how that happens.

Our bent shaft canoe paddles have held up like champs. The heavy backup paddles are still standing by, just in case we need to bludgeon a mastodon or something.

We've gone on smaller adventures, paddling, backpacking, and exploring rivers like the Neuse, Roanoke, and Cape Fear. I've recently joined the board of the New River Conservancy in their efforts to protect and maintain the river.

It was incredible to see that tiny creek in Minnesota swallow the waters of a huge portion of North America and transform into something massive. Cross over the bridge in a car, and you'll see just how big that thing is.

It was a hell of an adventure, but the trip of a lifetime? I hope not. We've still got more miles in us.

I wrote this book to document our experiences, and maybe inspire some kid out there to dream a little bigger and try something bold. I hope you enjoyed it as much as I did writing it.

Onward,
-John Pugh
September 15, 2025

P.S. By the way, did you know it is 3,503 nautical miles from New Bern, NC, to Cadiz, Spain, by sailboat?

Appendix
Resources, Gear, Contact

Gulf of Mexico
United States
Minnesota
Wisconsin
Michigan
Iowa
Illinois
Ohio
West Virginia
Indiana
Kentucky
Tennessee
Kansas
Missouri
Oklahoma
Arkansas
Mississippi
Alabama
Georgia
Louisiana
Texas
North Dakota
South Dakota
Nebraska
Lake Superior
Lake Huron
Lake Erie
Bay
Wawa
Sudbury North Bay
Sault Ste Marie
Barrie
Toronto
Hamilton
Buff
London
Sarnia
Detroit
Cleveland
Pittsburg
Bernidji
Lake Itasca
Jacobson
Fargo
Red
James
ck
rth
bota
uth
bota
rre
braska
Minneapolis
Red Wing
Fountain City
Madison
Milwaukee
Dubuque
Chicago
Des Moines
Lincoln
Springfield
Hannibal
Indianapolis
Columbus
Cincinnati
Louisville
Charleston
Kansas City
Jefferson City
St. Louis
Herculaneum
Grand Rapids
Lansing
Wichita
Cairo
Nashville
Knoxville
Charlo
Tulsa
Oklahoma City
Memphis
Little Rock
Friars Point
Greenville
Columl
Atlanta
Birmingham
Montgomery
Dallas
Sabine
Vicksburg
Jackson
Austin
San Antonio
Houston
Baton Rouge
New Orleans
Morgan City
Tallahassee
Jackson
Tampa
exas
Holston
G

ACKNOWLEDGMENTS

First, thanks to our families and friends, who not only humored the idea of paddling the Mississippi River but also stepped in with encouragement, supplies, and the occasional reality check when we needed it most. Amanda Allen, Donald and Britt Woolley, Betty and Kelly Fields, Candace McGuire, Chuck Milsaps, and countless others —your belief in us kept us afloat in more ways than you know. From the bottom of my heart, thank you.

We're grateful to the Audubon Society for shining a light on the importance of rivers and wild places, and to Great Outdoor Provision Company for their sponsorship and generosity. Their support reminded us that this trip was part of something larger than just two people in a canoe. It was about the shared responsibility to protect the waters and lands that sustain us all.

Sincere thanks to the *Greensboro News and Record* for publishing the series that helped fund the trip. Thanks also to Linda Munns, my high school English teacher, who took no crap, introduced me to Elvis Costello, and taught me how to string a few words together. And Matt Zuefle, my mentor and friend. Rest in peace, my brother.

To everyone we met along the river. Strangers who became friends, folks who offered a meal, a patch of lawn, or simply a kind word—you became part of the river's current that carried us south.

Finally, to those who couldn't be with us physically but were present in spirit, we felt you there the whole way. This book is for all of you.

-John

GEAR LIST

Canoe and Paddling

- Wenonah Minnesota II Canoe
- Bent-shaft paddles (2)
- Spare paddles (2)
- Life jackets (2)
- Bailers (2)
- Five-gallon water containers (2)
- Whistles (2)
- Compass, Map set
- Large sponge (2)
- Five-gallon buckets with screw-off lids (4)

Sleeping and Shelter

- Tent
- Ground cloth
- Sleeping bags
- Sleeping pads
- Sheet, fleece blanket (after Red Wing, MN)

Cooking and Utilities

- Cook pots and lids (2)
- One-burner propane stove
- Water treatment drops
- Weather radio
- GPS
- Repair kit (duct tape, needles, thread, superglue, etc)

- Clothing: pants, shorts, shirts, fleece jacket, hat, gloves, thermal underwear, etc.
- Sunglasses, rain hats, sun hats
- Sunscreen, lip balm
- Sandals
- Insect repellent
- Cell phones (2), PDA, micro-cassette recorder
- Notebooks for journaling, pens
- Books
- Hammock, Crazy Creek chair (2)
- Digital camera
- Toothbrush, toothpaste, toilet paper
- Wallet
- 50' parachute cord
- lighters (2)

First Aid

- Pain relievers
- Antacids
- Band-aids
- Allergy medication
- Misc creams and salves

SPONSORS

The following companies graciously donated products and services to the Source to Sea Expedition. We thank them from the bottom of our hearts for their support and commitment to making our world a better place. A special thanks goes to Great Outdoor Provision Company for their generous sponsorship and continued support of this and other endeavors.

Great Outdoor Provision Company
www.greatoutdoorprovision.com

Stolquist Waterwear
www.stohlquist.com
Wenonah Canoe
www.wenonah.com
Native Eyewear
www.nativeyewear.com
Pocketmail
www.pocketmail.com
Pacific Outdoor Equipment - RIP
Crazy Creek
www.crazycreek.com
Dr. Bronner's Magic Soaps
www.drbronner.com
Crocs
www.crocs.com
GSI Outdoors
www.gsioutdoors.com
Aloe Up
www.aloeup.com

Byer of Maine

www.byerofmaine.com

Annies Homegrown Natural and Organic Foods

www.annies.com

Jack Link Snacks

www.jacklinks.com

Lärabar

www.larabar.com

Organic Food Bar

www.organicfoodbar.com

West Soy Milk

www.westlifeplantbased.com

All Natural Peanut Butter & Co.

www.ilovepeanutbutter.com

Saco Foods Milk

www.sacofoods.com

Stretch Island Fruit Leather

www.stretch-island.com

Valley Fresh Kitchen

www.valley-fresh.com

Hodgson Mill

www.hodgsonmill.com

Sun-Maid

www.sunmaid.com

RESOURCES AND FURTHER READING

MISSISSIPPI RIVER PADDLERS

Bruce "Buck" Nelson
https://bucktrack.com/
Doing Miles - Amy and James
https://doingmiles.com/2014-08-mississippi-river/
First Church of the Masochist - Matthew Hengst & Jen Blackie
https://www.firstchurchofthemasochist.com
Ron Haines
https://ronhaines.org/canoeing-the-mississippi-river/
Dan Faust
https://dannofaust.wordpress.com/
Christine Thürmer
https://christine-on-big-trip.blogspot.com/

FACEBOOK GROUPS

Mississippi River Paddlers
https://www.facebook.com/groups/401767876586571
Mississippi River Angels
https://www.facebook.com/groups/2034967653391706
Lower Mississippi River Paddlers
https://www.facebook.com/groups/369247963153186

MAPS AND RIVER INFO

Minnesota Dept. of Natural Resources Maps
https://www.dnr.state.mn.us/watertrails/mississippiriver/index.html
Mississippi River Water Trail
https://mississippiriverwatertrail.org/
US Army Corps of Engineers Maps
https://www.mvr.usace.army.mil/Missions/Navigation/Navigation-Charts/
River Gator - Lower Mississippi River Guide
https://www.rivergator.org/

SELECT BIBLIOGRAPHY

Adventures of Huckleberry Finn, Mark Twain
Mississippi Solo: A River Quest, Eddie Harris
Kenny Salwey's Tales of a River Rat: Adventures Along The Wild Mississippi, Kenny Salwey
The First Hundred Miles are the Longest, John Shaffer
Bluffs to Bayous, Byron Curtis
Life on the Mississippi, Mark Twain
Ole Man (on a River), Ken Robertshaw
Rising Tide: The Great Mississippi Flood of 1927 and How It Changed America, John M. Barry
River Horse: A Voyage Across America, William Least Heat-Moon
Around the Bend: A Mississippi River Adventure, C. C. Lockwood
Down the Mississippi With Stinky: 2 Women, a Canoe, and a Kitten, Dorie Brunner
Floating Down the Country, Matthew G. Mohlke
River Journey, Clarence Jonk
Old Glory : A Voyage Down the Mississippi, Jonathan Raban
One Woman's River: A Solo Source-to-Sea Paddle on the Mighty Mississippi, Ellen McDonah

MISSISSIPPI RIVER CONSERVATION GROUPS

Audubon Society Mississippi River Initiative
https://www.audubon.org/our-work/rivers-lakes-wetlands/mississippi-river
Izaak Walton League of America
www.iwla.org
Upper Mississippi River Basin Association
https://umrba.org/
Friends of the Mississippi River
www.fmr.org
American Rivers
http://www.americanrivers.org

Mission Statement

In the summer of 2005, Jessica Robinson and I paddled over 2,150 miles down the Mississippi and Atchafalaya rivers in 73 days. We were both PhD students in Parks, Recreation, and Tourism Management at North Carolina State University. Our goal was to raise awareness for the Audubon Society's Upper Mississippi Campaign, which focuses on protecting and restoring critical habitats in the Upper Mississippi River watershed for birds, fish, wildlife, and humans.

Beginning as a small brook at Lake Itasca, Minnesota, the Mississippi gathers the waters of the Ohio, Missouri, and many smaller rivers, eventually emptying into the Gulf of Mexico some 2,350 miles later. Spanning between 1.2 and 1.8 million square miles, the Mississippi watershed drains 41% of the United States. It also serves as the primary migratory route for 60% of North America's birds.

During the journey, we utilized a variety of media outlets to spread the message, including writing newspaper articles and participating in interviews for print, radio, and television. We have been featured in several local, regional, and national programs, including National Public Radio's Morning Edition.

We are available for speaking engagements, sharing insights from the expedition, and discussing the importance of conservation and the Mississippi River watershed.

About the Author

John Pugh is an entrepreneur, avid adventurer, speaker, author, and trail advocate who has thru-hiked the Appalachian Trail and paddled the Mississippi River, and has over 6,000 miles of outdoor experience.

Passionate about how outdoor spaces connect people and strengthen local economies, John combines firsthand experience with research and advocacy. Whether hiking, paddling, or as a New River Conservancy board member, he's dedicated to showing how outdoor experiences build healthier, more vibrant communities. John is available to speak on leadership, resilience, and how lessons from the trail and river translate into success in both business and life. John can be reached at **John@SourcetoSea.net**

facebook.com/SourcetoSeaBook

instagram.com/houseofswank

linkedin.com/in/johncpugh

youtube.com/@SourcetoSea

tiktok.com/@house_of_swank

Upcoming Books

Keep Paddling: Business Lessons from Thru-Hiking the Appalachian Trail and Paddling the Mississippi River

*No Bullsh*t Guide to Thru-Hiking the Appalachian Trail*

*No Bullsh*t Guide to Paddling the Mississippi River*

The Mississippi River: A Photographic Journey

The Neuse River: A Photographic Journey

The Cape Fear River: A Photographic Journey

~

FIND A TYPO?

If you see a typo or other error, use this link instead of leaving a one-star review. Let's make the book better, together :)

https://bit.ly/S2STypo

THANKS FOR READING MY BOOK!

AND NOW, AN URGENT PLEA!

I really appreciate all your feedback and I love hearing what you have to say. I need your input to make the next version of this book and future books better.

Please take two minutes to leave a helpful review on Amazon, letting me know what you thought of the book.

https://bit.ly/SourcetoSeaReview

Thanks so much!
-John Pugh

Made in United States
North Haven, CT
02 November 2025

81751891R00126